About the Author

Wendi Schuller is a nurse, NLP and hypnotherapist. She went through a contentious divorce and learned many lessons along the way. She is a guest on radio shows. She has over one hundred published articles and is the author of "The Woman's Holistic Guide to Divorce." Ms Schuller is an avid traveller and has visited over sixty countries.

Wendi Schuller

THE GLOBAL GUIDE TO DIVORCE

AUSTIN MACAULEY
PUBLISHERS LTD.

A CIP catalogue record for this title is available from the British Library.

ISBN 9781785548413 (Paperback)

www.austinmacauley.com

First Published (2015)
Austin Macauley Publishers Ltd.
25 Canada Square
Canary Wharf
London
E14 5LQ

Printed and bound in Great Britain

Acknowledgments

Thank you to Soila Sindiyo of London, Founder of *The Divorce Magazine UK,* for her support and friendship. It is an honour to be a contributor to her stellar magazine.

I express my gratitude to two top solicitors in the UK for their legal contributions to this book. Austin Chessell is a Consultant Family Law Solicitor and Family Law Mediator in Knightsbridge, London. Anne Hall Dick is a Family Law Specialist and Family Law Mediator in Glasgow, Scotland. Their complete biographies are after their chapters.

Thank you to Dan Couvrette of Toronto, Canada, CEO of *Divorce Magazine* and *Family Lawyer Magazine*, for his advice and guidance.

I appreciate the many people who shared their stories and wisdom so that many others could have an easier passage through this turbulent time.

Introduction

The Global Guide to Divorce gives step-by-step advice on how to break the divorce news and what to do in the beginning, middle and post-divorce periods. This informative book contains insider's tips not found in any other any other source. True stories and examples are interspersed with practical legal, financial, and division of assets guidance to ensure the best outcome for divorce. Suggestions on how to select the best legal professional in your circumstance and where to find divorce resources are included. How certain personality disorders influence divorce and co-parenting are discussed. There are nuances between narcissists, sociopaths (anti-social personality disorder) and passive-aggressive spouses which can influence the proceedings. Knowing the intricacies on how to handle them in divorce and in co-parenting can make life much simpler.

Two top solicitors in London and Glasgow contribute information for divorce in the UK. Divorce processes for several different countries and the EU are summarized with important differences highlighted and extensive material regarding divorce in the United States is provided. The subtleties between divorcing in a community property state vs an equity one are explained. International divorce is complex and determining who has jurisdiction is mentioned.

I use my background as a nurse, hypnotherapist and Neuro-Linguistic Programming (NLP) practitioner to provide information and results of studies for health and well-being. Tips are given on how to stay in optimal condition during this frenetic period. Based on my experience as a school nurse, I describe how divorce affects children and offer suggestions on how to help them adjust to this transition. Emotional aspects such as forgiveness and increasing self-esteem are addressed. We started in the collaborative process and then my spouse dropped out, necessitating having to start over with new attorneys for litigation. He later agreed to pick up where we left off in collaborative divorce with our original attorneys. Ours was a divorce from Hell and the goal with this book is to prevent others from having a similar experience. Advice is spelled out clearly so others do not wander around in a fog as I did. Many people and divorce professionals kindly provided their anecdotes with wisdom to guide others along this path. Post-divorce we worked with a mediator who handled our communication and any children's issues. Options are presented on making co-parenting easier.

The Global Guide to Divorce deals with the changes in relationships with friends and family as well as in your new identity. It can be surprising who sticks with you post-divorce and who fades away. A chapter just for the guys deals with their particular issues and has links to resources for men.

The Global Guide to Divorce contains a section on doing a self-assessment before getting back into the dating scene. It gives tips for online dating and how to recognize red flags with new dates. Tips on getting through your former spouse's wedding day and being in a new blended family with step-children may be helpful too. My passion is travel and there are suggestions for traveling solo or budget friendly options with the kids. Facing holidays during divorce can be daunting so plenty of recommendations are given. Ideas for starting new holiday traditions either when alone or with children are shared. This book gives a blueprint to moving on post-divorce and thriving in this new phase of life.

1

Contemplating Divorce

Marital Counselling

Consider marital counselling if there is any chance of salvaging your marriage. Even if that does not solve the problems, then at least you know that you did everything that you could to save your marriage. If your spouse will not join you, then go alone. Marital counselling will provide support in this situation and guidance in taking the first few steps. My mother found it invaluable to have a professional confirm what she suspected, that it was time to bail, and she was given concrete measures to achieve this undertaking.

Problem: Finding marital counselling

Solution: Resources are available for marital and individual counselling in your community and even online. Your physician may be able to refer you to a practitioner and word-of-mouth is another good way to find one. Check online for client satisfaction reviews.

• Alternatively, there are charities globally that provide relationship counselling which increases couples' interaction skills. Relate is UK based, and provides couples' counselling for marital problems. Individuals are welcome and can receive assistance in deciding whether to leave a marriage and how to do so. They have counselling for children, gay couples, plus partner with other charities in this field. Relate's councillors go through an extensive training provided by this organization. In Scotland, Relate is called Relationship Scotland. Since Relate is a nonprofit group, the counselling fees are kept at a reasonable rate to make it affordable for all. Relate also has workshops to enhance relationships. Singles are welcome, so they can learn skills to strengthen a future marriage. Relate is very accessible and will do counselling by telephone, e-mail and online. One can click onto their website and chat with a counsellor, which enables this charity to be far reaching.

• Retrouvaille is sometimes considered the last hope for saving a marriage and preventing divorce. Couples may be in such despair and pain that divorce seems to be the only option in ending this misery. Some American clients are sent there by judges and attorneys as a prerequisite before divorce. Retrouvaille means "rediscovery" and is a charity that teaches tools, such as communication, to enrich relationships. "Established in Quebec in 1977, Retrouvaille weekends offer couples an opportunity to learn about listening, forgiveness, communication and dialogue by working closely with married couples who have faced similar challenges." In 1982 Retrouvaille came to the states, and in 1991 it spread globally. It starts out as a weekend session and continues for three months after this. The three month follow up is necessary in continuing to implement these new skills. The focus is on improving communication and if divorce is inevitable, clients will be better able to have more effective interactions with former spouses. It was started by the Catholic Church and couples of all faiths, plus atheists are welcome. Three married couples and a priest run the weekend sessions. A minister and spouse would replace the priest when it is for Christian Multi-Denominational (CMD).

If you are dead sure that you want a divorce, please do not drag your spouse to marital counselling. Have your own private sessions if applicable. One lawyer couple's marriage was breaking down and the wife was not clear why this was happening. She pushed for marital counselling and the husband agreed to a weekend with Retrouvaille. Barbara was hopeful after their return and was stunned when her husband left immediately. He had a young girlfriend with her two small children waiting for him, and he filed for divorce that week. It was cruel to give Barbara hope when he was already planning to leave the marriage.

Pre-Divorce

It is imperative that you have a credit rating in your own name before you divorce. Get a credit card in your name only, and do not have any co-signers on it.

This was the main way that I was able to survive during my divorce, before my interim support started a month or so later. Take some money out of a joint account and open one in your name. If this is too difficult, then open an individual account with some loose cash from around the house. Check the number of your credit score to get a sense of potential borrowing ability.

It is important to have access to money to get you through the initial stage of divorce. A friend who sensed I was heading for divorce before I did, gave me a nice gift card to a grocery store as a Christmas gift. When their marriages were on the rocks, a few women bought gift cards for themselves to use at a later date.

Document any marks, such as bruises, even for occasional beatings. Although it was only a few times a year, one father would grab his son so hard that a bruise would form on the boy's arm in the shape of his fingers. The interim psychologist during the divorce turned that father over to the Children, Youth and Family Department (CY&FD). He hired a high-priced attorney who was able to get the investigation closed quickly. CY&FD told the mother that if she had had a picture or two of those bruises, the outcome could have been different.

Many people feel it is prudent to consult an attorney when even contemplating a divorce, to obtain astute legal advice and invaluable guidance that can help prepare you for whatever problems that might arise during the divorce.

Records and Financial Statements

If you have the time while you are contemplating divorce, then get your financial records and assets in order. Go to your bank and get copies of transactions from your personal and joint checking and savings accounts. Get copies of any pension plans and IRAs showing the contributions. Order the last three years of tax statements from the IRS and your state. There is a list in the back of the book of what to give your attorney. Peruse this to see what financial records are needed. It will give your new attorney or mediator a fuller picture of your situation, if these records are available at the first visit.

Look in files at your co-owned business before divorce and make copies of financial records. Right after my ex left me, before the staff was notified, I swooped into our jointly owned business and quickly grabbed what records and personal effects that I could, but only when I knew that my husband would be not be there

Ensure that your name is on the deed to your house. In community property states, you still may be able to get your share of the house, even if it is solely in your spouse's name. In the UK, the Land Registry can let you know if your name is on the house deed by doing a title search. If it is not, they have a form to fill out to register as co-owner of it.

Anabel, her husband, and their two children had lived in their house for over a decade. During their divorce, Anabel received a nasty surprise. Unbeknownst to Anabel, her in-laws legally owned the house and theirs were the only names on the deed. What she thought had been mortgage payments over the years were essentially deemed rent. They had no other large assets to split in their divorce, since each of their vehicles was worth about the same amount.

Her husband had lost his job and was living off income from a family trust, which further complicated alimony and child support. Check deeds, investments, and other assets to ensure that your name is on them. Anabel did not start out well post-divorce.

Whether or not one is in a rocky marriage, they should put inheritance or family money gifts into a separate, not a joint account. Do not mix these with other joint accounts or assets. If you do mix them together (co-mingling), you usually lose claim to them. In a divorce situation, when kept in a separate account, inheritance and your family's money gifts are considered personal property, not joint assets. Keep in mind that joint accounts, such as checking, can be frozen when one spouse passes on, even when in the middle of a divorce.

Selecting a Divorce Attorney or Mediator

Decide, before hiring a divorce attorney, if you want a courtroom divorce a collaborative one in the lawyers' offices or mediation. Some attorneys do only one type of divorce and others also do mediation. Word-of-mouth is a great method of finding the right divorce attorney. Approach people that you know or do business with and inquire whom they would recommend. Ask divorced people in your social and professional networks whom they hired for their divorces and if they were pleased with the service.

An employee at one retail establishment, whom I routinely did business with and valued his opinion, was insistent that I hire a particular attorney. Her name started coming up on other people's recommended lists also. I hired this attorney and was quite pleased with my choice. Check the Better Business Bureau and State Bar

Association to see if your selected attorney has any complaints against her. Go online and look up her profile and law firm. Who's Who publications rate the top people in a particular field, including law. Some attorneys specialize in high profile or celebrity divorces. Others have a niche representing a spouse when there is extreme wealth. These attorneys' fees would be high, so may be too expensive for routine divorces.

Denny picked an attorney who is one of the nicest, most mild-mannered guys you could ever meet. He is someone you would like as a friend or neighbour. Unfortunately for Denny, this fellow was way too laid back in the court battle with his wife's shark-like attorney. The wife got quite a lot in the divorce, including a big chunk of Denny's business. Instead of a marriage partner, Denny now had an overbearing business partner. When selecting an attorney, make sure to verify the attorney's demeanour in the courtroom.

Sometimes one or more names of lawyers who have gouged clients are mentioned. My friend's legal fee in her divorce was the exact amount that she received for her share of the marital home. One divorced man said to see if anyone mentions sleazy lawyers, so that you know whom to avoid. Just as a great attorney's name may keep popping up, so can a less ethical one, too. During his divorce, he and his wife agreed to a personal property settlement. One of her girlfriends kept telling his wife "you can do much better." Well, the wife got her attorney to ignore the settlement agreement and go after more goods. The judge upheld the original agreement, and the only thing more the wife received was a much larger bill from her attorney. Her lawyer had the reputation of doing what he could to inflate his clients' fees.

In another case, a woman told her attorney just to settle the divorce, because she just wanted to be done with it. Yet it dragged on and on. She contacted her husband, and to her surprise, he had told his attorney the same thing. Her attorney kept "stirring the pot" to get higher fees. Together, the spouses got the divorce finished more quickly by having a united front when working with their attorneys, who completed the details.

A divorce tip for the ladies from my acquaintance, Lenny, is that guys are "programmed to just want to get the divorce over quickly, unless there is anger or revenge involved."

Listen to your intuition when selecting legal representation. Trust is an important element in this relationship. A pleasant lawyer couple that I did business with before my divorce just did not seem right. I would meet one or both of them for coffee or lunch. I felt sorry for the woman, because she did not seem to have any girlfriends. Their billing was lumped into days, rather than by hours, so I was probably charged a lot for my misguided sympathy in meeting that attorney for what I thought were social get-togethers.

This couple also did some estate work for my mother, but did not want us to come to their office, even for a quick signing of papers. They insisted on meeting us at my office. My mother kept asking them if we were being charged for their time commuting, but she was repeatedly given vague replies. I rue that I did not mandate a breakdown by time, so I could see whether or not we were charged for unnecessary commutes.

If you are not pleased with how the attorney's bill is structured, then speak up. Rather than having a total amount for a day or week, have it broken down by tasks or time periods. The statement could say 2:00 pm to 2:30 pm answered and sent emails, $125. Went over records and reports from 3pm to 4pm, $250.00 with the date. In this manner, you will know that your bill isn't being padded. I prefer having the time slot and what work was performed during that period. Stating fees hourly would have indicated if that attorney had been charging for chatting over lattes. I would have ceased these immediately and possibly fired her.

Maybe there are expenses that you can control better, such as ceasing to send unimportant emails. Each phone call or e-mail is an additional charge, unless you have a package deal for a divorce. Doing your own work of going through bank or investment statements can save on the cost of a paralegal performing these tasks. Some friends have consulted up to four of the best divorce attorneys in town, in order to purposely prevent their spouses from being able to hire these esteemed legal minds. While some attorneys offer a free initial consultation, these savvy women opted to pay the fee instead, thus establishing the confidentiality of a client-attorney relationship. This guarantees that their spouses will not be able to have these lawyers represent them, if their husbands should call their offices at a later point. If you have paid the fee to establish this private client-attorney relationship, but opt not to hire that attorney, then what is said to her or the office staff cannot be used against you later in a divorce situation by your husband. Unfortunately, this works the other way, too. In one case, when a husband already had a girlfriend and wanted out of the marriage quickly, he went to the best divorce attorneys in that city to prevent his wife from hiring them.

In a particular case, a couple planned to move to another city and intended to commence their divorce proceedings at that destination. Unbeknownst to the wife, the husband made a quick trip for interviews with that city's top divorce attorneys. After the move, the wife got quite a surprise when the attorneys said that that they had already been interviewed by the husband. Finally, one agreed to take her on as a client. The husband's interview had been so brief, that the attorney did not consider it a client-attorney relationship. Had her husband plunked down the cash for these initial meetings, then that relationship would have become official. The other advantage to meeting several lawyers is that you can select the one who clicks with you best. It is important to feel comfortable with your attorney and be able to work together as a team.

First Attorney Encounter

The first point of contact, after the secretary, will be the paralegal who will get your contact information and listen to your story. She will check with the firm's attorneys to make sure that there is not a conflict of interest in accepting you as a client. If your chosen attorney, or possibly another partner, had any dealings with your spouse, they may not be able to accept your case. The paralegal will ask some questions to clarify your situation. The next step is that she may get the attorney on the phone for a brief encounter or just to schedule a face-to-face meeting. You may be asked to bring a retainer fee in a certain amount to your first meeting or dropped off soon afterwards. See chapter on raising cash.

At your first meeting (or may be instructed to deliver these beforehand) bring the following documents and information:

Any bank and financial statements, including tax returns.

Your children's' social security numbers and financial records.

Your pre-nup agreement, if applicable.

The history of your marriage. Any affairs? Did you hire a detective?

Any alcohol or drug abuse? Any mental illness?

Any physical, or emotional abuse?

The complete list is in a section in the last part of this book

Have a list of questions and concerns ready for your first meeting. She may answer some of them in her introduction, then just cross those off your list. Having questions on paper will help you to be more organized and not leave thinking, "Why didn't I ask that?" Areas of consideration are:

Estimate of cost of divorce

Expected time frame of divorce or number of sessions in collaborative

The amount for interim support

How will visitation work?

Who is paying the household bills during divorce?

Take notes during your first meeting, to review later, when you are less stressed. This information made my initial encounter go smoothly, and enabled my attorney to quickly grasp my situation.

I called my attorney within a few days of our first meeting regarding changing the locks. Contact your lawyer first and get permission before changing the locks after your spouse has moved out of the marital home. Two nights in a row my sons and I heard a person moving around in our house in the wee hours of the morning. The locksmith and alarm company came out that day and changed locks and all alarm codes, including my garage door opener. If getting a restraining order, your attorney may have you do this immediately. If not sure whether it is a burglar rummaging around at night, keep safety in mind and call 911 in the US, 999 in the UK, and 112 in the EU.

Divorce Sessions

Keep notes of the divorce sessions, as a secretary does in club meetings.

Make notations of compromises made, since recording is prohibited. Jot down questions to discuss with your attorney after each session. If there is a statement that you do not understand, get immediate clarification. This is not the time to assume something only to find out later that you misinterpreted it. In my collaborative divorce, one attorney would send a group e-mail of the important points made in the meeting. Carefully read it for any crucial omissions or inadvertent mistakes. If your head is spinning with too much information, feel free to ask for a break. Just nipping into the ladies room to do quick stretches or deep breathing helped me to get back on task.

2

Resources in Divorce

Call your United Way to see what community resources are available to you. Other good sources to contact are a women's health centre or the local community college. Ask specifically for support groups or classes for women or men getting a divorce. Some cities have men's groups, such as the *Talking Sticks* in Surry, UK which provide camaraderie and support, although not specific to divorce.

In the UK, contact *Maypole Women*'s charity which supports "women before, during, and after separation and divorce." They have links to helpful resources and can also assist with formulating an exit plan before separation. Online support for divorce and beyond are *The Divorce Magazine UK, Divorce Magazine,* and *DivorcedMoms.com* which have great articles for both genders.

`An online search for *Dads' Group* lists many in locations around the world who provide valuable support and advice. *Men's Divorce News* has a plethora of information and a weekly newsletter. *The Next Chapter 4 Women* gives step-by-step guidance both pre and post-divorce.

The Lilac Tree in the Chicago area, will meet with women individually to assist them in finding the right resources for their particular situation. This non-profit offers support groups, workshops and seminars to empower women and offer education during the divorce process. Another divorce organization, *Visions Anew* in Georgia, also offers workshops and seminars. They assist in bringing divorcing people and professionals together.

The Divorce Center in Massachusetts provides professional development for divorce professionals as well as seminars for divorcing spouses. They also have parenting classes. Do an online check to see what classes, support groups, and non-profits are in your area. Sometimes a one-time divorce workshop may be offered in your city. Check upcoming events regularly.

The Women's Center in the Washington D.C. area has two locations that provide counselling services. They also run classes such as the six week course, "Finding Emotional Strength During Separation & Divorce."

Your friends are a great resource for advice. Emma told me that there is a "light at the end of the tunnel," and that the pain of divorce diminishes. Kelly wished that she had reached out to friends and learned this piece of wisdom at the beginning of her divorce: "I would have liked to have known that the pain would eventually go away." When caught up in the maelstrom of divorce, it would have been difficult to realize that life gets better, without my friends' words of wisdom.

Pets

What do you do if one is moving into temporary digs and cannot bring a pet? Contact your local humane society, animal rescue group, or animal shelter to see about getting your pet enrolled in a foster program. I volunteer for a cat rescue group and we found a temporary home for a cat that was owned by a service man being deployed to the Middle East. This cat had a loving family until the soldier returned. In the UK, RSPCA can arrange for a foster home during divorce. Their "PetRetreat" program particularly focuses on families who are in an abusive situation and require temporary homes for pets.

Needing a Place to Stay in a Hurry

An option, which started in London and has spread to other countries, is Homeshare. This charity matches a companion or caregiver to an elderly person who wants to stay in her own home. The companion swaps a little help for no or low rent. It can be cooking supper and watching a bit of TV afterwards for part of the evening. Having a person staying in the home gives the senior citizen a sense of security, while benefiting a person going through a divorce, too. This is a commitment, and is not for those wanting a place for a brief period.

Go online and check places such as Craig's List or holiday apartment rentals in your area for a temporary place to stay. Let people at work and other places know that you are seeking lodging. If family is nearby, some have moved in for a few months or more until financially back on their feet.

The YWCA is an international organization that empowers women and girls in various ways. Some YWCA buildings have low cost apartments for women to live in during transitions. Services, such as getting a GED, treatment for addictions, or just help getting employment is available

Women in Transition Course

Some community colleges have a course named "Women in Transition," which is excellent for recent widows, empty nesters and those going through a divorce. The class meets for around three hours a week and the women have a confidentiality agreement (written or oral), where everything said in the class stays there. Women can discuss their most personal feelings, relay traumas and receive understanding from their supportive classmates and instructors. It is a safe environment to express oneself and to gain personal insight.

The "Women in Transition" course features at least one speaker a week on a myriad of subjects, ranging from fitness to finances and qualifying for a mortgage. The CPA discussed ways to elevate our credit rating and erroneous actions which lowered it. The psychologist was excellent and gave concrete strategies for managing stress, including court hearings. She gave practical tips on how to deal with difficult people in our lives. We had some homework between classes, which increased our awareness and problem solving abilities regarding our personal situations.

The support and friendship from the classmates makes going through heart-breaking, stressful situations a lot easier. I felt less alone in my divorce when others shared their experiences. These classes run six to eight weeks, and people often want to stay in touch after the class ends. Even if you feel that you have it all together, please consider enrolling in this valuable class.

There are support groups for men and women that meet regularly to discuss various issues. If there is not one specifically for divorce, it still can be worthwhile to check out this type of assistance. In the movie "Starting Over" with Burt Reynolds, Candace Bergen, and Jill Claiborne, there are humorous scenes with both men's and women's support groups. The movie really shows the difference between genders in an enjoyable way.

Unfortunately, my lawyer did not know of any support in the community for folks going through divorce. Others lawyers that I discussed this with were also unaware of the "Women in Transition" course. Do not rely on your attorney to help you in this area.

Abuse Situations

Another source for guidance is your local Rape Crisis Centre. Ours does free counselling for adults and children who have been in abusive situations. Domestic violence is easier to spot when one has visible wounds, rather than emotional or financial abuse. Financial and emotional abuse often go along to together. Financial abuse is about control. One spouse is attempting to control the actions of the other by taking away their financial independence. Sometimes an abusive spouse takes the other's name off a bank or checking account so that person has to beg for cash. That spouse may demand to see receipts and keep a tight lid on money. He/she is controlling the relationship through money and handouts.

In one case, a woman inherited a little bit of money and put it into a separate account. She was in a bad marriage and her husband was enraged that she had more independence with this fund. He removed her as being able to sign checks in their jointly owned business, which was their main source of income (financial abuse). He took over paying bills, since the money used for them came from their business. Their house then went into foreclosure, they received disconnect notices from the utility company, and their credit cards began to accumulate interest. The abusive spouse wanted his wife to either beg for money or to deplete her inheritance as a way to control her. The wife was doubting her own competence. Months later they got a divorce and the wife felt a sense of freedom.

Emotional abuse is about perceived power to keep the other spouse in line by manipulation and humiliation. The spouse is put down and their self-esteem and self-worth take a nose dive. They may doubt their own intelligence and competence. When children witness this abuse, they may see the parent on the receiving end as weak. This challenges that spouse's authority with the kids. If a wife is having some success, then the husband may want to put her in her place by lying, threats, and blame. This is a specialty of Narcissists.

Even if children are not direct recipients of abuse, they still suffer from the effects. Children may repeat patterns of witnessed abuse. Females might become submissive and marry an abusive spouse or males may be violent with their families. They may become bullies to other children if they have received physical or sexual trauma. I have seen this both in schools and in a large children's hospital when they were undergoing therapy. Unless intervention is done, it is possible for kids to continue this familial cycle of abuse with their own offspring.

When children cannot or will not talk about abuse, then it can manifest in physical ways, such as bedwetting or developing asthma. Dr. Robyn T. Cohen and other researchers from Brigham Woman's Hospital and from Harvard stated, "Our findings highlight the importance of screening for asthma among victims of childhood abuse and to be aware of the possibility of physical or sexual abuse among children with asthma."

The Rape Crisis Centre does great work with Post Traumatic Stress Disorder (PTSD), teaching concrete strategies for dealing with the triggers. Adults and children from abusive marriages can have PTSD, and it is imperative to receive help to avoid, or learn to minimize, its triggers. The Rape Crisis Centre greatly assisted me in decreasing my insomnia and enabled me to minimize stress in post-divorce courtroom hearings. They even sent a support person (advocate) to go with me during an especially difficult court hearing post-divorce. My sons both went there post-divorce for short-term therapy to heal a specific issue.

Higher Power in Divorce

Many people find that their religious faith is a source of comfort and guidance during turbulent times. Jen said that she reads the "Book of Psalms" when she has questions or strife, and opens the Bible and points to a random verse. Invariably, it contains just the answer that she was seeking. Carrie is currently going through a divorce and became more active in her church, doing the Gospel readings during Mass. In lieu of a support group, some women have opted to join a ladies' group at their place of worship. I have met some wonderful ministers' wives who embody the concept of unconditional love and who listen to many confidences.

Some have turned over their divorce problems to God/ Higher Power and got a sense of peace. Valerie did this with great results. She had a son with an abusive man and wanted to leave him and go back to her family across country. She discussed this situation with her woman's prayer group. Valerie was astounded to receive several thousand dollars that these wonderful ladies had quietly collected for her. She left the south and is happily living in Chicago and providing for her son. Valerie is one of the most joyful women I ever met. It is important to take the path that feels most comfortable for you.

3

Breaking the News

Problem: How to inform one's spouse about wanting a divorce

Solution: Chances are that your spouse will not be caught off guard by the announcement of wanting a divorce. If you are going to marital counselling and made the decision that divorce is inevitable, seek their guidance. The counsellor will help to formulate a plan of how to discuss this with your spouse. Perhaps, you could have a session to inform your partner with the counsellor present. This will not be easy, but it is better to get it over with so that you both can start to move on.

Karla and her husband had casually discussed their mutual unhappiness and possible parting of ways several times in the past. He is nineteen years older and this age difference added to their troubles. Karla calmly in a matter-of-fact voice, stated that it was time to divorce. Wendell thought about it for thirty seconds and readily agreed. This low key, respectful way to make the announcement set the tone for an amicable split.

• There are different ways to accomplish this and each situation is unique. Do not break the news with the kids nearby. They do not have to be in the periphery of this drama. Perhaps have the grandparents watch them for the evening. One woman did not like having her husband give her upsetting news in public. Sitting in a restaurant, then having to make a mad dash to the Ladies Room while tears were streaming down her face, made it much worse. She kept asking "Why didn't he just tell me at home?"

• Know what your boundaries are. Your spouse may beg for another chance or berate you. Have some responses ready in your head, so that you do not cave in or make a decision in the heat of the moment that you will regret later. Be prepared for your spouse trying to get you to feel guilty. You are in charge of your emotions, so choose not to feel guilt. He/she may say that you are tearing up the family and harming the kids. If the situation becomes heated, say you are willing to discuss it at a calmer moment, although you will not be changing your mind.

• Use "I" statements to get your message across without assigning blame to the other person. For example state, "I have been unhappy for a long time..." or "I have been feeling frustrated and need..." Do not say "You are such a jerk, overspent, and you make me so angry." Remember that you have control over your emotions and reactions, so your spouse cannot "make" you feel something (anger, hurt). This is taking responsibility for your feelings and what you require to do about them (divorce).

• Let your spouse hear about the divorce directly from you. Do not tell other people first, who inadvertently may let it slip. If you suspect possible violence or retaliation, make sure your pets are somewhere safe. One woman's healthy kitten died mysteriously when her angry husband was alone with it. Organizations, such as Maypole Women in Leeds, UK helps with this situation. Take precautions for yourself and children and get advice from your local Domestic Abuse organizations for what steps to take. An attorney can advise you on how to extricate yourself from an abusive spouse.

• Janis decided to split personal property and assets before informing her husband that she wanted out of her marriage. She took half of the furniture, linen, kitchenware, and decorative items out of the house. Her next stop was the bank where she withdrew exactly half from their savings and checking accounts. She saved these receipts to show what she took. She did not have to break the news verbally, because her livid husband figured it out. Another woman, did something similar. Anne prearranged with her friends to bring over a small moving van after her husband left for work. She took most of the furniture and household goods, the majority which had been hers before marriage. She had another place already rented and moved in with her small daughter. Anne's attorney informed her husband of the pending divorce. This is not the recommended way of informing one's spouse, but it worked in these two situations with volatile spouses.

Problem: What to do when you are on the receiving end of divorce news

Solution: It may come out of the blue that your spouse is leaving you for someone else, or for another reason. Even if you had suspicions, it is still a shock. Your whole life has changed in the space of a few minutes. Realize that you are in shock, same as hearing about a death, and get some help. Some people have described this as an out of body experience, where they felt numb, but their bodies carried on with necessary tasks.

• Try to collect yourself first and feel free to ask questions: Could we go to a marriage counsellor? Why did you not discuss your unhappiness first? Are you having an affair? For how long? Resist the urge to throw furniture or light a bonfire and burn your spouse's clothes (a suggestion given to me). A violent reaction could impact your divorce case.

- If your spouse urges you to move out of the marital home, resist unless it is an abuse situation. Seek legal advice first before moving out, especially when there are children.

- After your spouse departs, consider a mad dash to the bank to withdraw some cash (no more than half from a joint account and save the receipt) for living expenses until interim support kicks in.

- Call a family member or close friend to be with you. Do not try and make any major decisions, just process your roller coaster emotions. If you suspect your spouse may drain your joint assets, then contact an attorney to have them frozen. This is why it is important to have a credit card in your name and your own bank account. Get an attorney soon to take care of urgent financial issues and to set up interim (temporary) support.

- You may want to take a few days off work, however some throw themselves into their jobs to keep panic thoughts at bay. The important thing is to nurture yourself, with rest, nutrition and pleasant distractions. Meet with a divorce coach, clergy, or trusted family friend to get some guidance. If the sudden announcement of one's spouse wanting a divorce leaves a person incapacitated, have a loving, neutral person, like a godmother, take the kids for a day or more. They will have positive support, an ear to confide in, plus maybe some fun diversions. This gives you time to regroup.

• I took an already planned trip with my mother and sons to Hawaii during the beginning of divorce, and that was just what I needed. The palm trees, ocean breezes, and quirky shops took my mind off my misery. This trip set the tone for my divorce: chill out and enjoy life. I never would have gotten back on track without this trip in the middle of chaos. Both attorneys agreed that my spouse could not go, even though he had tried to replace me on this vacation. The interim child psychologist declared it was just what the boys required. An artist on Maui crafted a small Tiki statue for me that represented strength and carved "Adventures Forever" on its back. He reassured me that I would do fine in my divorce. If one can take even a few days for a trip, it really does rejuvenate you. Laughing at others' outrageous divorce stories makes yours seem more mundane.

Amada's mother booked a trip for them and her two teenage daughters before the divorce commenced. Amanda's husband was going camping with his buddies during this period. When the divorce started, these four were allowed to take the prepaid European river cruise. Amanda and her daughters returned refreshed and were more relaxed during the rest of this collaborative process. She was surprised at how empowered she was after this journey which positively impacted her divorce. Even if you take several day trips to a neighbouring city or park, it can get you out of your distressing surroundings and do wonders for your psyche.

Problem: How to Tell Children about Your Imminent Divorce

Solution: Tell your children at home and not on vacation or visiting someone else.

One child received the news at summer camp and the counsellors and new campers had to help her deal with this crisis. This was a convenience for the parents and quite cruel to the girl. At home, the kids have the opportunity to take comfort in their rooms or confide in the family pet. Our cats listened, purred, and cuddled with my boys.

• You may want to break the news of your divorce to your children with your spouse present, reassuring them that they are loved. By both of you. Explain that details have yet to be worked out, but they will be able to spend time with each parent. Do not pass blame onto the other parent, even if a third party is involved. State the facts as calmly as possible.

• A seventeen year old boy told me that having a lead up to a divorce conversation is helpful to kids. One night his parents got in an argument and right afterwards told his brother and him that they were getting a divorce. There had been no previous arguments or warning, so receiving the news bluntly was a shock. Think about mentioning that you both are working on some problems and at a later date delivering the news of divorce.

• Make it very clear to the children that they are not responsible in any way for the divorce and this is an issue between both spouses who will work together to make the divorce smoother for them. Reinforce to your children that they are not to blame for the divorce. Do not put down the other parent. Perhaps just avoid talking about him or her in general. Children know that their other parent has faults and they do not require them to be catalogued. Under no circumstances say, "You are just like your father." It serves no purpose, even if you mean it as a compliment. I knew that my father had issues and my mother periodically stated, "You are just like your father." This got me wondering if she thought I was nuts too.

• Give the kids time to express their feelings and to ask questions. Feel free to say you both will get back to them with more specific replies when not sure what an answer is. They just want some reassurance that their lives will have some constancy. One teen stated that his parents did not affirm that he and his siblings would be okay. He suggests that parents address this when breaking divorce news and let kids know they will be fine.

• There are some wonderful children's books on divorce written for specific age groups. You may want to have at least one in your home to give out after your announcement. A great one for children ages seven to ten is *When Love is Broken* by Soila Sindiyo. She has written a series of books for different age groups.

• Have a family friend on standby so children are able to vent their hurt and sadness to an understanding third party.

I was the recipient of a "Dear John" note that the children and I both read. I could not reach my husband by phone, but was able to contact his mother, who confirmed the contents of the message. Ideally, you and your children do not find out about your husband's departure at the same time. I do not know if I was more surprised by the note itself or by my sons' happy reactions to it.

In-laws and Parents

You may want to tell your parents privately, plus also have a chat with your in-laws. When spreading this news, set the tone on how you want others to respond.

Surprisingly, I vacillated between shock and euphoria, so I presented the news in a positive frame. Friends acknowledged my shock and gave me nurturing, positive support.

When one is in shock, it is difficult to perceive how others are reacting to the news. Some parents may be doing the happy dance, if the marriage had been an abusive one. Others feel like they are losing a beloved family member and have to process their emotions first before being supportive. Parents may express anger since their world is changing and they have no control over it. Tell your parents explicitly how they can help, such as babysitting or informing the rest of the relatives. Some do better when they have these specific tasks to do. If one's parents seem clueless, perhaps revealing the uglier parts of your marriage will put them in the picture. If your parents are expressing their disappointment, it is fine to tell them that you have to leave and will talk to them later. Getting on the defensive is not going to help your psyche, but taking a short break will.

During your divorce, consider pulling back from your in-laws to create space. If you love your husband's family and want to continue your relationship post-divorce, keep your divorce details private. They may feel conflicted because "blood is thicker than water." They also could reveal confidences which may add to the divorce conflict. The in-laws may feel that their son is being unfairly persecuted, so keep mum.

If your in-laws are not abusive, reassure them that you want them to continue to be an important part of your children's lives. Grandparents can be invaluable with providing a loving, neutral space for children. It is in everyone's best interest when grandparents can give non-judgmental support to kids during this difficult time.

Your in-laws may feel caught in the middle between two warring parents. Let them know you value their relationship with the kids and will inform them of school, sporting and other events. This will put you in a good light while fostering your children's bond with their grandparents.

Grandparents

Help your children continue special traditions with both sets of grandparents, whether it is baking holiday cookies or planting spring flowers. Continuity is greatly supportive in your youngsters' changing world. Grandparents can also be involved with the kids in simple ways, such as buying a product your son's school is selling, so his class makes their quota. Remember to have kids send "Happy Grandparents' Day" cards. My elderly friends regularly told their former daughter–in–law that they were her backup babysitters. When they went out of town, they called her with their temporary replacement. Her family lived out of state so she made sure these wonderful people stayed closely involved with their grandchildren.

I had a standing date with my mother for her to watch the kids on a designated day every week after school. With this free time, I could make plans in advance to meet friends or just have a chunk of time to do errands without dragging cranky children with me. Perhaps this arrangement would work out well with your parents or former in-laws, and the kids are guaranteed regular contact.

Unfortunately, some grandparents may choose to sever all contact with their grandkids. In one case, the grandfather was very passive, and during visitation, his wife would loudly proclaim the perceived faults of the boys' mother. Due to paternal abuse, the older son stopped visitation and the younger one had court-mandated supervised ones. Eventually, the younger son was allowed to stop his visitation. The grandparents told the boys that they would only have contact if they resumed a relationship with their father. Luckily, the boys had a wonderful, loving grandmother, plus other elderly family friends who filled the vacant positions.

Mutual Friends

A tricky situation is how to deal with mutual friends. Your spouse's co-workers and college alumni will align with them. Be careful with couples where you are friends with the wife and your spouse with her husband. Your friend may inadvertently pass along juicy tidbits about your situation to her husband, who then tells your spouse. You may share what is happening in your divorce to your golfing buddies while out on the links. They in turn may pass along some confidences to their wives who gossip to yours. This could gum up the works in a contentious divorce.

I did call some of the spouses of my husband's colleagues at the beginning of our divorce. I thought it was best that these women heard the news from me directly, particularly since he wrote that "Dear John" letter. This interaction made it much easier to chat with these ladies post-divorce, although we did not formally socialize again.

Be cautious with whom you share your divorce details. People do talk and may not realize that their co-worker or neighbour knows your spouse. This could come back to "bite you in the bum," as my attorney warned.

At a women's luncheon, I discussed my pending divorce with two women whom I know did not pass along anything. However, someone eavesdropped and called my husband, who was furious, and brought this up at the next divorce session. I permanently dropped out of that organization and learned not to discuss private issues in a public setting. At least have a code name for your husband, so an eavesdropper does not realize whom you are referring to when speaking in a coffee shop or store.

4

Divorce and Costs

The majority of states have both no-fault and fault grounds for divorce. No-fault is when there is a breakdown of the marriage or incompatibility. In this type of divorce, no one has to point a finger at the other party. In the states that have fault divorce it is due to cruelty, adultery, impairment, abandonment and desertion. Other grounds are for what was not revealed before marriage, but were discovered afterwards. This list includes impotence, infertility, homosexuality, imprisonment and incurable mental illness. The grounds for divorce globally are discussed in later chapters in this book.

Collaborative

The collaborative method was developed in 1988 and specified as collaborative law in 1990. Collaborative divorce arrived in the UK in 2003. Family law attorneys receive additional training in the collaborative process. Collaborative divorce takes place in one of the attorney's conference rooms with the attorneys and spouses present. The negotiations involve give-and-take in a more pleasant atmosphere, often with lattes and pastries. Instead of having one person (judge) make the decision, the outcome of issues is decided upon by the four people present. The solutions are immediate, without waiting weeks for a judge's ruling.

In between meetings, the spouses consult with their own attorneys. What is different about the collaborative process is that the attorneys discuss the case with each other. They work together in the collaborative process so that spouses can agree upon the outcome of various aspects of the divorce. If one spouse is especially difficult, the two attorneys are a team in keeping that party in the collaborative process. The lawyers are trained in recognizing body language, so may call for a break if it looks like one person is about to lose it. It is allowable to speak to one's own attorney privately during the proceedings.

Impartial experts are brought in as needed during the sessions, especially the financial advisor. These people on the divorce team are described in a later chapter. The meetings may be as often as desired, including weekly or bi-weekly as opposed to months, as in the court system. Collaborative divorce can be finalized in several months for uncomplicated circumstances and settlements.

Collaborative divorce is especially good when one party is well-known and the other one is not, and for celebrity couples. Judges are supposed to be neutral, but can show favouritism. Collaborative does away with this factor in divorce.

Confidentiality is important in collaborative divorce and what is said cannot be used later, if a court divorce is desired. What has been said in the conference room stays in the conference room.

If one of the spouses is abusive or toxic, collaborative divorce can still be done. The spouses can be in separate rooms with the attorneys going between them. If I came early, I waited with the paralegal in her office until all had arrived. I sat at the opposite end of the table from my spouse and I gave him at least a ten minute head start before I left the attorney's office at the end of the meeting.

If one of the spouses decides to back out of collaborative proceedings in the middle (like my ex), then the whole divorce has to start completely over. The attorneys and expert advisors cannot take part in the court proceedings and new ones are hired. One starts from ground zero and the money spent on the previous proceedings is lost. Luckily my spouse decided to go back to collaborative and our original attorneys agreed, and we picked up where we had left off before. My spouse's attorney said that ours was the most difficult divorce that he had ever experienced.

Litigation in the Courtroom Divorce

In this type of divorce one is putting their fate into the judge's hands and wishing for a good outcome. The person who initiated the divorce is the petitioner and the other spouse is the respondent. The petitioner's attorney presents their case first before the judge, followed by the respondent's. A contested divorce is when one party is opposing the divorce and it usually ends up in court. Non-contested is when both parties agree with getting a divorce, but not necessarily agreeing with all aspects of it, such as division of property.

The first stages of litigation are determining both the actual complaint and what one hopes to attain from the divorce in assets and support. The papers are then served to the other spouse. One couple was on very good terms and mutually decided upon a divorce. They had discussed their marital situation, realizing that they would get along better as friends than spouses. The husband was quite shocked and upset when his wife had divorce papers delivered to him at work, in front of clients and co-workers. He stated that all his wife had to do was to call him and he would have fetched them. This set the tone for an adversarial divorce. If you are on the receiving end of divorce papers, read them carefully.

The following stage in litigation divorce is the discovery, where all assets are put on the table. Financial records and other information are shared between attorneys, so that the property can later be divided. Negotiations may end in a settlement, and if not, the divorce case goes before a judge, who makes the final decision.

In divorce, one presents monthly expenses, and a temporary amount will be paid by the higher earning spouse. This is called interim support. In litigation, the court may freeze assets so that they cannot be sold, cashed in or hidden. As in collaborative, litigation will impose some restrictions, such as not changing the beneficiary of a life insurance policy. You are probably the beneficiary pre-divorce, so this prevents your spouse from changing it to their new love interest once divorce proceedings commence. If they die mid-divorce, you then are protected.

If an agreement is not reached, then you and your lawyer next prepare for court. Whoever initiated the divorce appears first before the judge. The other party follows, presenting his/her side. After the evidence is presented and expert witnesses are heard, then the lawyers present their legal arguments. The petitioner's attorney presents her case first before the judge, followed by the respondent's. The judge then makes a ruling (decision), which is the divorce decree.

Testifying in court can be traumatic, and the other spouse may have a "winner take all" attitude. Adversarial divorce may close the door on exes working together post-divorce on various issues that might arise. It can make co-parenting more challenging when spouses have battled it out in court.

Some husbands and wives have felt that the court system gave better results for their divorces. One man's wife was a model who had been unfaithful. He filed for a fault divorce using the ground of adultery. The judge told the adulteress to take her clothes and personal items out of their house. The husband wound up with everything else. He would not have gotten such a rich settlement if he had used the collaborative process and was quite happy with the outcome of his court case. Depending upon where you reside, a court judge may be more sympathetic to a spurned spouse.

Some people choose litigation when their spouse wants them to receive nothing in assets. They are told that is what they deserve since the divorce is their fault. A judge would mandate that assets be split. Others are divorcing spouses with personality disorders who refuse to negotiate, and would not participate in mediation or collaborative divorce.

When one spouse is insisting upon full physical custody and painting the other as an unfit parent, either might choose to go to court. In the UK, a Cafcass officer who is a family advocate, interviews the children, parents, and other pertinent people and gives a report to the judge. A spouse may want to go through the court system with Cafcass involved in custody recommendations.

In an abuse situation, a person may not want to see their spouse in a small conference room or the spouse refuses to compromise.

Costs Involved with Divorce

The average cost of divorce in America is $15,000 in 2014. In the UK, a contested divorce is on the average £5000 to £20,000. An uncontested one starts around £1300. Particularly in England there are many package deals on divorce, depending upon whether you are initiating it (petitioner) or the recipient (respondent). One solicitor web site in England had a package special for the respondent for £600. Do a web search in your area for prices on the attorneys' web sites and you can contact them for estimates or hourly rates. The above UK prices are for divorces without children. Litigation is the most costly type of divorce. In the UK, a barrister may be required for court and that bumps up the legal fees.

With both types of divorce, you will be required to pay a retainer to your newly hired attorney, and in my case, I paid $5,000. Collaborative divorce is a lot less costly than a court divorce. There are typically four to seven sessions before the divorce is finalized. It can take over a year to complete a litigation divorce. After I paid the initial retainer, subsequent payments to my attorney were taken from "the community pot," not from me directly. As property and other assets were sold, the consultants and both attorneys got paid, and the leftover money was divided between us. I was out of a job during part of the divorce, since we had a jointly owned and run business. The money that came into the business during our divorce was still a community asset, so some of the lawyer's fees were taken from that. This is particularly good for stay-at-home moms or working women who make significantly less that their husbands.

An option is to hire your own personal financial advisor to check over this aspect of your divorce. Although there may be one already working with both attorneys, it may bring you peace of mind to have your own adviser to go over details with you between meetings/court dates.

Mediation

Mediation is gaining in popularity as another option to complete a divorce, at a fraction of the normal cost. The mediator is a neutral person with extensive training in negotiation, who works with both the husband and the wife to divide assets and complete the divorce process. Just as with the other types of divorce, spouses bring financial and tax records, plus any other pertinent information to these meetings.

At the first meeting, you will go over rules, just as in collaborative sessions, such as no threats, yelling or recording the sessions. Goals will be discussed and you will be asked about your relationship and the desired outcome of the divorce.

Both of you share financial information and whatever else the mediator requires.

Mediation does especially well in amicable divorces, where the spouses may want to stay in touch afterwards. In mediation, there is more dialogue, so everyone has a better comprehension of the reasons behind what each spouse wants. This gives the three of you a better understanding of each spouse's positions, so that compromises can be reached. A mediator works with both parties together, typically in three sessions. A fair distribution of assets and resolution of other issues are accomplished within these sessions.

You do not have to go it alone through mediation, but can have an attorney guide you from behind the scenes, although not at the sessions. You attend the mediation sessions with just your spouse. Your lawyer can give you advice and also review any documents from the mediation negotiations. It is possible to just hire an attorney to review the final contract before it is signed. This saves a bundle of money, because you get the benefit of an attorney's advice and strategies without paying for her time in the actual mediation sessions.

Financial advisors can look over the preliminary financial and alimony settlement before you signing anything. They can guide you from the side-lines and advise what retirement benefits to get or what are the more advantageous assets in your circumstance.

In the States, mediators charge from $150 to $500 (California) per hour. A mediated divorce can cost from $800 to $7000, depending on your locale and how complicated your divorce turns out to be. This can be the cheapest type of divorce. In the UK, the average price for mediation is £675 per person. On April 22, 2014 there was a law passed in the UK mandating couples to have an initial mediation consultation (for most cases) before pursuing a divorce through the court. This allows spouses to see if mediation is right for them, thus keeping costs down and reducing the backlog of cases in the courts.

In the US, the norm is for one mediator to meet with both spouses for the divorce meetings. In the UK, sometimes two mediators preside over the divorce negotiations. This is particularly done when one spouse is "overbearing" as was stated at a Family Law Mediation conference in London. An experienced London solicitor who also does mediation, estimated that 30% of his cases for divorce are done with a co-mediator.

Do it Yourself Divorce

A couple with a non-contested divorce (both parties agree to it), who wants to do it on the cheap can get the required documents plus legal advice online for only $299. The price is 100% refundable if the court does not accept these divorce papers. There is a comprehensive guide and step-by-step process to enable you both to complete this task. There are other online sites offering free divorce forms.

Some companies will do the paperwork for you.

In the UK, spouses can do DIY for simple divorces, which are non-contested and no children under sixteen. Many solicitor web sites have these DIY kits and will look them over at a set price. DIY divorces run from £69 to £150. It is possible to get free forms online from sites such as The Ministry of Justice. Court Clerks also have DIY forms. If people need assistance filling these out, contact the Citizen's Advice Bureau (CAB). The CAB and Gov.UK have websites that explain the divorce process.

A friend bought a book with legal advice and divorce forms. She offered to take a little less of their joint assets, just to get her husband to agree to file for divorce in this way. She nabbed a judge in the hallway and the whole process cost her $75. Her husband had family wealth and she did not want an expensive court battle with his high-priced lawyers. She may have gotten alimony if she had had a more traditional divorce, but was willing to give that up just to get out of the marriage quickly and cheaply.

Residency and Domicile

Countries and states have a minimum period for residency in their locale before divorce can be initiated. It can be six weeks, as in Nevada, or one year like in New York. The average period of residency before being able to file for divorce is six months. One may have to show utility bills, landline phone bills, and other proof of residency in that state. The term residency or habitual residency is where you actually reside. Only one place can be designated as habitual residency.

Domicile is a tie to a certain state or country, but not necessarily living there at the time one wants to file for divorce. It is a legal connection to a country, such as having a passport. A Londoner can have an internship in California, but file for divorce in England (domicile). People who are married from different countries, may petition one country for divorce where a spouse has domicile (born and raised). A couple from America and Sweden can petition for divorce in Wales after residing there for a year, or file in one of their countries. Go to a solicitor who is experienced in international law to advise the best course of action in a situation like this one. If a couple files for divorce in a different country, an attorney knowledgeable in international law can make sure that the divorce is recognized in their countries too. It is imperative to seek legal advice in deciding which country to file an application for divorce, if living abroad. Some strictly divide assets down the middle and others may give one spouse, with less earning ability a bit more.

In England, Wales and Scotland, the habitual residency period before filing for a divorce is one year. Say a Canadian couple moved to the Scottish Highlands, they would have to reside there for one year before being allowed to file for divorce. One does not have to have a legal connection, such as family there, in order to petition for divorce. If one also has domicile, then they (petitioner) can file a petition for divorce after six months, instead of a year.

Different places may have a minimum time being married before divorce can be initiated. England and Wales require one year, yet Scotland has no time mandate. In the US, there is no minimum time to be married before filing for divorce. Drew Barrymore's marriage to Tom Green lasted 166 days.

Desertion

It is possible globally to get a divorce when one spouse has deserted the other one, although the terminology differs for it. In the UK, desertion comes under "Irretrievable Breakdown" of marriage. In Scotland there is no desertion, but rather would be considered non-cohabitation for two years with one spouse consenting to divorce. One must attempt to locate the missing spouse to serve divorce papers at the last known address. If the papers come back as undeliverable, then contact friends, relatives, last known job or professional group. The key to getting a divorce with desertion, is documenting these attempts to find one's spouse. This is particularly true when married to a foreign national who may have returned to his or her country of birth. After being granted with the divorce decree from desertion, one is free to remarry.

Ingrid's husband deserted her and their children. She knew that he had done drugs in the past and guessed that he assumed that lifestyle again. She was young and did not realize how to track him down to get child support. Much later she was served with a final divorce decree. Her husband spent many years in prison and that was the main reason he was out of the picture. He got engaged and his fiancée did the paperwork for his divorce. After the divorce was finalized, wife number two found out later where his ex-wife lived and had the papers sent to Ingrid.

In cases of desertion, it can be painful when the parent and children reconnect. There can be rejection and angry feelings that require processing before moving on. In this case, the oldest son wanted the father back into his life, but the father was having difficulty in this situation. When this good student asked for a small sum of money to buy college text books, his father baulked and said that the son only wanted money (not true). Family counselling is a good place to start when healing broken relationships.

Annulment in America

Hollywood marriages lasting only a few days may end up being annulled. Britney Spears' marriage to Jason Alexander lasted fifty-five hours. An annulment is similar to a divorce, with the difference that after an annulment, it is as if the marriage never happened. It becomes null and void. Grounds for an annulment of short marriages include fraud: one spouse was not told certain facts about the other person. This includes a prison term, having a sexually transmitted disease or being impotent. Another more popular category for an annulment is mental illness or being incapacitated at the time of marriage. Many of the Hollywood celebrities have used this, claiming that they were drunk or impaired and did not give proper consent to marriage. This is not downing a few shots before the ceremony, but rather being inebriated and getting married quickly afterwards, perhaps with an Elvis impersonator conducting the nuptials. If you were deceived, or at least one of you was impaired going into the marriage, it may be possible to get an annulment instead of a more costly divorce.

Annulment in the UK and Commonwealth Countries

Annulments are less likely to be granted in the UK, than in America. There is no waiting period to apply for an annulment, as there is for a divorce. The criteria is similar: bigamy, having a sexually transmitted disease when wed, and the marriage was not consummated. The woman not telling the male that she is pregnant with another's child, is considered another act of fraud. The process takes six to eight months. There are legal packages for uncontested and contested annulments costing at least £ 1900.00. People do not have to appear in court for an uncontested divorce in the UK. What bumps up the price for an annulment is that they do have to appear in court. If granted, the marriage becomes invalid, as if it never happened.

In Scotland, there is no formal annulment process. The court can deem the marriage invalid and the couple can then remarry others. The criteria for having the marriage declared void is similar to the ones in other countries.

Canada grants an annulment only if the marriage took place in that country. Similar to the UK, court appearances are mandatory for an annulment, and not for an uncontested divorce.

In Australia, the term is "nullify" is used to indicate that the marriage is void. The marriage does not have to have taken place in that country. It can be obtained if one spouse is Australian (domicile) or both live in Australia as a permanent home (residency). One spouse serves the other with an application for a marriage annulment. They have twenty-eight days to file an affidavit to contest the annulment. If there is no response in that time period, then the court will still hear the case. An annulment may be granted if there are grounds for it, even if the other person does not show up in court.

Annulment in the Catholic Church

A Catholic annulment is getting easier to obtain these days primarily on the grounds that the couple was not prepared, or did not understand the full extent of this sacrament. If they entered into matrimony very young or with unrealistic expectations, annulments have sometimes been granted. Grounds that make a marriage invalid are: one partner did not fully consent, lack of maturity and understanding of marriage; not having the intent to be faithful; and not being open to having children.

James is a devout Catholic who married Betty also a Catholic. They went to the required Pre-Cana (pre-marital counselling) classes, plus met once with the pastor of the church where they were to be wed. He felt that their values aligned and they agreed on basic issues. Two years into the marriage James was shocked that Betty was being unfaithful and decided to end their marriage after consulting with a priest. The priest said Betty's behaviour was between her and God and James could not change it. The priest encouraged James to apply for an annulment so that he could get remarried in the Catholic Church in the future.

The process for a church annulment is straightforward, but lengthy in time. One spouse files a petition for an annulment and the other one has the opportunity to agree or contest it. Both spouses choose or are assigned a representative to make sure their side is heard during this process. This can be clergy or a lay person who interviews and assists the former spouse. Both spouses fill out a lengthy questionnaire regarding their dating and marriage history. Two witness for each spouse then fill out forms as well. The witness must have known the person before the marriage. This goes before a formal Tribunal of judges who assess the information presented and consult with the two representatives. After a year to eighteen months, a determination is made. Both spouses are then free to remarry in the church. If an annulment is not granted, both spouses could still remarry in a civil ceremony. There is a fee for the annulment process, but can be waived if someone cannot or will not pay it.

5

The Divorce Team

Financial Advisor

The attorneys will obtain a financial adviser, who is especially qualified to work in divorce cases, to go over your joint assets. She will be invaluable in digging through financial records and fairly dividing these assets. Everything is laid out on the table, including the blue book worth of your vehicles. Loans are tricky and may be put on one person's side, if he will be getting significant property later, once the loan is paid. Or all loans may be paid off, including credit cards and mortgages, and the difference given to the spouses at the conclusion of the divorce. It is in your best interest to fully cooperate with this adviser.

This financial adviser will probably attend all of your divorce sessions, unless one is specifically for visitation. She will draw up lists of assets and assist with the determination of interim support. There is a formula for alimony and child support based on income, so she may help less in this area. She may be the one paying joint bills from the community pot, such as to workers renovating a jointly owned house being prepared for sale during the divorce. Money from assets sold during the divorce is put in a trust fund, and checks are issued for joint expenses from this account. Bills are paid to lawyers and advisers, and for work being done to get assets sold.

If she finds that some assets appear missing or if there are questions, then a forensic accountant or even an investigator may be hired. Sometimes a forensic investigator is used in determining personal and business assets to make sure everything is on the up and up. Your spouse may have transferred money from your joint account to a friend or relative. If he/she does jobs where they get paid in cash, look into the existence of a safety deposit box. In one divorce, a husband was flashing his wad of hundreds at his son's school. The forensic accountant was unable to solve this mystery. In some cases of wealth, there may be a hidden off shore bank account.

Interim Child Psychologist

The lawyers may want a child psychologist on board to set up interim visitation. She may initially meet both the parents and the children to get a sense of the family dynamics. In a contentious divorce, the parents have individual consultations, where the children are met separately. The psychologist does not do therapy, but may give suggestions or strategies to enable the children to have a smoother transition between parental homes and to teach them how to deal with visitation. She monitors visitation to make sure that the situation is suitable. At the beginning, behaviour expectations are announced, such as the parents not putting each other down and limiting divorce discussions in front of the kids. If there are any violations or issues, these are addressed.

The interim child psychologist may recommend to the attorneys and parents that the children start therapy with another psychologist. Also, if abuse is discovered, then the child psychologist is bound by law to turn over the offending parent to a child protection agency, so they can make an official determination.

Before or at the beginning of your divorce, ask around to see if there is a particularly good or less effective child psychologist. I found out the hard way that four other mothers would have loved to tar and feather the interim child psychologist that our attorneys had jointly selected. She was the sweetest person, someone you would select as a new best friend. However, this psychologist saw the world through "rose coloured glasses," a bit out of touch with reality. She looked and acted the part Amy Adams played in Disney's "Enchanted" movie. This professional wanted overnight visitations when the boys could not handle short daytime ones. If she had determined custody, it would have been a disaster.

Most likely, the court or the interim psychologist will mandate that both parents attend a parenting class and may specify a certain one. The parents attend them at different times to avoid conflict. I got more out of listening to the other parents and how the instructors helped them deal with individual situations than I did with the actual content taught. It was so helpful to hear the fathers' perspectives regarding visitation, divorce proceedings and other issues. I gained a wider understanding about many things. The camaraderie was great, and this was a safe place to vent and gain self-awareness.

Children's Therapist

Both parents have to agree upon a psychologist to do the therapy for the children. Again, do a word of mouth survey, or ask your paediatrician whom she recommends. I highly urge you to find a psychologist who is strong, and who would be willing to go to court, if necessary, for your child's best interest. My sons' therapist has gone to court several times post-divorce, as an advocate for my younger son regarding visitation. A mother, who also had a bad time with the same interim psychologist, had suggested this therapist, who stepped in during her divorce and changed the visitation schedule for her son. I was very glad that I followed her advice.

The therapist will continue therapy in the post-divorce period for as long as the children need it. My older son stopped before his younger brother. The Parenting Plan stipulates the percentage that each parent pays for this after divorce.

Custody Evaluator

It may be that you and your spouse agree upon visitation times with your attorney's support. The interim visitation schedule set up by the psychologist may work all right and custody can be based from this. However, if it is unsatisfactory, then the attorneys may get a formal custody evaluation performed by a qualified psychologist (one who does this regularly for the court). This is a good way to proceed, if you feel that custody and visitation arrangements are not going well. Talk to your attorney about bringing this professional on board. We had to pay the custody evaluator $8,000 up front, and the whole process took several weeks, with a binding parenting plan issued.

The custody evaluator meets with the parents together for the first time, or separately, in abusive situations. She will spend time interviewing each parent to obtain a marital and parenting history. I gave a copy of the one I did for the initial meeting with my attorney. Then parents and children will do a battery of personality tests, including the MMPI (Minnesota Multiphasic Personality Inventory). It is important to answer these questions honestly and not how you think the custody evaluator would expect. One young man lost out on a job by answering these questions by how he thought they would make him look great, not by how he actually felt and perceived himself. He failed this personality test and was not asked for an interview. Not answering honestly will backfire.

The Rorschach inkblots test is where one creates a story to go with a picture. A psychologist said to pick the happier image for these types of personality tests. If several images come to mind, select the amusement park over the apocalypse one. A similar test is making up a brief story to go with a picture. Before doing any of these, get in a calm state of mind first. Take deep breaths, meditate, or watch a comedy, whatever helps you get in a good mind-set before embarking on these tests.

Parents will have a chance to refute any allegations made by the other spouse and state their wishes for custody. You and your attorney will meet with the custody evaluator, and so will your spouse and their attorney at another time. The recommendations will be presented in the parenting plan.

Life Coach

Your attorneys, or the interim psychologist, may recommend that one or both of you see a life coach to talk over your concerns and make sure you are on the right path. A life coach does not do therapy, but rather helps you problem-solve if you feel stuck. She can help you form concrete strategies, such as how to go about looking for a job. She may have you draw a circle (pie chart) and divide it into different aspects of your life, such as time spent doing various endeavours. This helps you gain perspective on priorities if one segment of your life is greatly diminished.

It is easy to get off track during divorce and a life coach can give you a reality check. If you are caught in the blame game, she can help you gain insight into how your actions contributed to the divorce. A life coach supports your efforts in forging new relationships and trying to make sense of the old ones. A life coach may be allowed to come to divorce hearings in order to give you support.

A Divorce Coach is a Life Coach who specializes in this area. She can give a clearer picture of reality when a person is stuck and cannot see how to move on. A Divorce Coach may work with children to assist them in adjusting to having two homes. She can be invaluable post-divorce when issues and frustrations arise.

Career Coach

There is a new member on the collaborative divorce team who is the career coach and is becoming an invaluable asset during negotiations. Quite a few women have put aside their work aspirations to raise a family and have been out of the job market for a while. A career coach may be brought in to help these women determine their strengths and weaknesses to develop a plan of action. An initial assessment of skills and interests is performed, and then the woman and career coach investigate potential jobs and career paths. It may be that the woman has developed new areas of interests and accomplishments from her previous jobs and requires some vocational guidance during and post-divorce. The career coach can assist with concrete tasks, such as helping to write a resume and check job wanted ads. Another function is to provide reassurance and support for the spouse who is now hunting for a job.

An additional reason that a career coach is brought on-board is to help determine alimony and child support during collaborative divorce negotiations. These are determined by the earning potential of both spouses. If one spouse has to go back to school or get training to update her skills or license, then the career coach can point this out for a fairer alimony/child support settlement. In an acrimonious divorce, the career coach is a neutral person who can help assist with alimony in an impartial manner.

6

Custody

A custody evaluator will write a parenting plan which is entered in court as part of the divorce decree. Sole Custody can be granted to one parent when the other parent is abusive or impaired. The courts across the country are moving away from granting this type of custody in deference to Legal Custody to both parents. In Sole Custody, the one parent has complete say in the child's decisions and does not have to consult the other parent. If one parent is completely out of the picture, then this is when Sole Custody is more likely to be awarded.

Legal Custody is usually granted to both parents, and this allows them to make decisions regarding the child's medical, educational, religious, and schooling, even if one parent is in jail. The incarcerated parent can still have input on the child's upbringing. When a parent is an alcoholic or drug abuser, then visitation may be supervised, but Legal Custody can still be awarded. If a parent makes important changes, such as a school, the other parent can take that parent to court if he had not been consulted in this decision. Although my children had visitation, I was reprimanded for not informing my son's father that our child had gotten a job during our divorce.

Physical Custody is granted to the parent where the child completely or predominately resides. This may be that the child lives with his mother during the week and stays at his father's house on the weekends. It also is awarded to a parent when there are no overnight visits or in cases where visitation is supervised. Joint Custody is when the child spends part of the week at each parent's house or alternates every other week. It may be close to 50/50 and often the parents live nearby to make it easier for the child's schooling.

The UK is more progressive than the US in realizing that 50/50 shared care is more in the parents' best interest, than the child's. Assets can be divided down the middle, but not necessarily a child. There are more frequent transitions which can be upsetting to kids, as I have heard numerous times as a school nurse. Ever hear a school kid mutter that he doesn't really have a home? (50/50 split). Polling other school nurses gives these same answers. Some kids do okay, but I have found that more do not with equal shared care. The famous American child psychologist John Rosemond states this against having 50/50, "Going from one home to another every few days…is disruptive. Going from one home to another every couple of weeks (with more extended stays on special occasions) is still somewhat disruptive, but much less so."

Instances of where family members, other than parents, are awarded custody are becoming more common. This is particularly the case when both parents are impaired or incarcerated. Then grandparents, aunts or uncles may be granted custody. I personally am seeing this more and more in the public schools. I am having to call a grandparent or guardian to pick up a sick child or ask an aunt to obtain permission to administer a medication.

Shared Care time for custody arrangements is a work in progress at first and may need to be tweaked to suit the child's needs. Keep communication open with the kids to prevent problems with it from developing.

Parenting Plan

The parenting plan is a written record of what parents or the custody evaluator have decided in regards to most aspects of the children's lives. It spells out the amount of shared care which is the percentage of time to be spent at each parent's residence. It includes how holidays, school breaks and vacations are to be split. It may be a simple document, or very detailed in regards to schooling, activities, and parental behaviours not allowed. In acrimonious divorce, specifics, such as neither parent talking about the other parent, can be addressed.

The parenting plan may stipulate the percentage that each parent pays for therapy and medical bills. For example, I paid 33% of them and my former spouse's share was 67%. In some countries and states, the parenting plan is a court document which is legally enforceable, and in others more of a suggested guideline.

If parents are having a contentious divorce, the parenting plan may appoint a mediator, listed as the "court monitor," to handle all communication between the parents post-divorce. He sends or forwards emails, such as trips planned and any other communication. In many divorces, the other parent has to be informed if the children will be taken across state lines or out of the country. If, when a child reaches eighteen and does not want to continue visitation, the court monitor deals with this situation, notifying the other parent, and possibly finding a person to supervise the younger one's visitations.

In a case where the two sons had no contact with their father, their mother only had to notify the court monitor of the trip date and itinerary. The court monitor then sent these details via email to the father. Definitely work out these issues during a divorce, so there are not acrimonious court battles afterward.

It may also prevent either parent from calling Children's Protective Services on the other one, but instead, may have complaints go through the court monitor to determine justification. If there is a basis for an allegation, then he would contact the appropriate agency.

Whether it is stipulated in the parenting plan or in the divorce decree, address college expenses. Make sure that your spouse will pay for all, or least a certain percentage of tuition, room and board and other fees. Have it stipulated that this includes grad school as well. If your higher earning spouse balks at having to pay college expenses, be creative. See if they would do a lump sum after high school graduation, paid directly to the university. This could be a tax write-off. Or maybe they would be willing to open a 529 plan for each child, which is a savings account that is for a child's educational expenses. My husband only would pay child support until each son's high school graduation and nothing beyond that. If you are facing this, do what my attorney did and stipulate the month and year of the high school graduation when child support ends.

Amy, a divorced friend's daughter, decided to graduate early by the GED route. Then she enrolled in cosmetology school. Since Amy finished school a year ahead of schedule, her father stopped child support early. He refused to pay any tuition for cosmetology school, even though she was still under eighteen. The attorney did not specify an ending date for child support.

If you want to stay put, and the other parent is dreaming of living across country, consider addressing the issue of moving in the parenting plan. There could be a clause in it stating what high school the kids are to attend, as was in my parenting plan. If you want to prevent a move, it is easier to say something along the line of, "kids remain in this city until high school graduation." At a much later date, it is hard to know how a judge would rule on this issue of moving, particularly when one parent is from another country. There have been some shocking rulings in the news. Judges have ordered that children go to another country with a parent, when they do not even know that language. If you want to relocate near family, then this may not be possible.

Tonya moved away from her family and friends in Fresno to live in Reno with her new husband. Things were great until they had kids. Her husband refused to change or cut down on his travel or work hours and saw very little of Tonya and their offspring. They divorced, and Tonya could not move with the kids back to Fresno, or even go for a long weekend without her husband's permission, as per the divorce decree.

An unfortunate new trend is to mandate reconciliation, or also called reunification therapy, with an abusive or estranged parent, after the parent has undergone counselling. This process is formally set up with each person having a different therapist to work together to achieve this endeavour. Strongly oppose this, because if the children want to have a reconciliation with the abusive parent, this is possible without being mandated by the court. In one case, more abuse was revealed by both children after the divorce. Yet, one nutty judge tried to enforce the parenting plan, by mandating that the reconciliation therapy still take place.

The younger child was still in visitation, so it was costly for his mother and time intensive for the child's therapist to thwart this court ruling. Luckily the child's appointed reunification therapist refused to take part in this travesty, when it clearly was not in this boy's best interest.

Parenting Class

In an acrimonious divorce in particular, a judge or the attorneys may mandate that parents attend a parenting class. There are videos and discussions about the material and how it pertains to real life situations. There are tips for making future co-parenting easier for all involved. In parenting classes one learns not to have the children pass messages to the other parent during visitation. Kids feel put on the spot, especially if these youngsters know they are the bearer of bad news.

If you are required to take a parenting class as an aspect of your divorce, but you cannot find babysitting or work crazy hours, here is an option. Inquire if you can take an online parenting class that gives a certificate upon completion. An excellent one for parenting plans and tips on successful co-parenting, is the one by Soila Sindiyo through udemy.com

7

Divorce Negotiations

The Judge

Judges are supposed to state any connections with either party or their families. In some states, judges hearing cases are not allowed to be friends on social media with any person involved in that lawsuit. You might want to check on this or ask the judge point blank if he has any personal dealings with your spouse or their family. I had a judge who immediately told me that she knew my ex-spouse's parents and asked if I wanted her to recuse (dismiss) herself from the hearing. I said that I was okay with her, as long as she felt that she could be impartial. I appreciated her honesty upfront.

When Toni went to court, the judge looked vaguely familiar, but she could not remember why. This judge limited Toni's attorney to making only a few statements, and would always rule in her husband's favour. Toni's attorney was quite flabbergasted by the judge's behaviour and ordered transcripts of the court proceedings to verify this issue. Toni started telling people about this particular judge to see if anyone else had had the same experience. One acquaintance was floored and said, "He cannot be your judge because he is John's buddy." It turned out that Toni had met the judge earlier in her marriage, and had witnessed various interactions between these two men. She notified her attorney who filed for a hearing to have this judge recuse (dismiss) himself from any future court hearings. The judge did recuse himself, although was very defensive about his socializing with Toni's husband. If you feel that you or your spouse have previously met your judge, do some research to verify that he and your husband are not lodge brothers, college alumni or in some other social situation together.

Linda and her husband were getting a divorce in a western state. Her husband was able to get new judges when things were getting sticky and not going in his favour. Linda felt when each judge got to actually know her husband and realize that he was being a jerk, then that judge was replaced. On the fifth go-around, Linda got fed up with this game and took action. One is not supposed to write to a judge, but Linda sent a short note explaining that he was now judge number five. At the beginning of these divorce proceedings, this new judge explained that he would not be stepping down at any point for a successor.

Insurance

You may want to have the children remain on the other parent's insurance plan as part of the support package. See if this coverage can be extended through college or at least until they are twenty-one. Have your lawyer state that the children's insurance plan cannot be changed without your consent. This became important post-divorce for me. The plan that my ex has includes one doctor visit a year without co-pays, plus pays for part of medications. He wanted to change it to a plan with co-pays, which meant I would be trying to collect what is due me more often. I vetoed this idea. Your spouse will be unable to change to an inferior health plan, or one with a higher deductible or co-pays.

During your divorce, any life insurance policies may have to be cashed in and used as an asset to be divided. My husband's life insurance policy was bought and paid for during our marriage and netted $58,000. This money went into the community asset pot, which was used for collaborative fees and to renovate our house for resale, with the remainder split between us. Whoever is paying child support may be mandated to take out a new life insurance policy in at least the amount that covers future alimony and child support. Make sure you are listed as a beneficiary and get a copy of this at least once a year. After your divorce, if you are the one paying alimony/child support, be sure to remove your ex as a beneficiary from your insurance and name another person(s).

Passport for Minor Child

There are a plethora of subjects to address during divorce proceedings that make life easier down the road. If your child's passport is up for renewal or a new one needs to be issued, then have your spouse sign a notarized letter right then and there giving permission to obtain a new one. There is a notary in every attorney's office. If you had an acrimonious divorce and now you want to take your child out of the country, this could be a touchy situation. If your child is under sixteen, then *both* parents and child must go to the passport centre together, with the necessary documents. If this is not feasible, then one parent may give notarized permission for the other parent to obtain the passport for their child.

The US passport Agency will allow a judge to write a statement granting permission for just one parent to obtain a passport for a minor. This could be the judge who presided over your divorce case. Your teenager can petition the court herself for the right to allow one parent to obtain her passport. This is what happened when a fifteen year old legally changed his name and required a new passport. When his father refused to participate in his passport renewal, he asked the same judge who consented to the name change to write a note on official stationary permitting only his mother to get his passport. It worked. When you take your child out of the country, have a notarized permission letter from the absent parent. I carried an e-mail from the court monitor that my ex-spouse had been informed of the trip. If you have the passport in your possession and the other parent asks for it to plan a trip, be careful if you think that there could be a risk for kidnapping. Consult your lawyer if you are in this particular circumstance.

Quit-Claim Deed

A quit-claim deed terminates a person's claim or interest on a property (grantor). The property transfers to the recipient (grantee). In divorce situations, when one spouse receives the marital home, then the other spouse often signs a quit-claim deed to make a clear transfer of it. This does not release responsibility for future mortgage payments for the grantor if both spouses' names are on the mortgage loan. If the grantee reneges on the mortgage, then the loan company can go after the grantor who signed the quit-claim deed. Often, the grantee is required to refinance the house solely in her name during the divorce proceedings, to prevent this possible scenario for the husband at a later date. If you sign a quit-claim deed in your divorce, make sure your name is removed from any outstanding loan on the property.

Sometimes a quit-claim deed is signed to prevent any trouble at a later point. When Elena bought her husband out of his share of a house jointly owned with her mother, the divorce lawyers had the husband sign a quit-claim deed. The house was completely paid, so no need for refinancing. Her mother owned a small house out of state, so the lawyers had the husband sign a quit-claim deed on that as well. The husband had no ownership interest in that house, but Elena's lawyer did not want the husband to try to cause any difficulties post-divorce when the mother died. I bought and closed on a house during my divorce. Even though the house and mortgage were only in my name, the attorneys had my husband sign a quit-claim deed on it.

Karen's parents started a lucrative clinic where she was a doctor. Although her husband had no interest in this business or employment there, Karen's parents still insisted that he sign a quit-claim deed in her divorce. This protects the business if the ex-spouse tries to claim some compensation at a later date.

Getting a Job during Divorce

Before my divorce, I was forced out of my job in our jointly-owned business. My attorney insisted that I immediately find employment. Besides earning a little extra cash in this part-time position, it helped me keep my sanity and enabled me to have more power in my divorce. Since it was far less income than co-owning a business, it most likely gave me more leverage in my alimony amount. One hurdle with determining alimony is that it can be calculated on what you potentially earn, even if you have been out of the work place for many years. It is a toss-up if bearing with even a lousy job during divorce helps with increasing alimony, but it can also boost self-esteem by proving that you can still find a place in the current job market.

The April 11, 2013 *New York Times* magazine section had an article by Judith Warner that discussed returning to work after a long hiatus when one was rearing children. A question was raised as to whether it is better to get a job during the divorce or to wait until it has ended. A divorce attorney told his client, "Before you do anything, you get a job. You have to look at the next ten years of your life, and if you're in control of the situation, and you have a job that's paying you money, he's going to be far less powerful over you in the divorce."

Social Media in Divorce and Beyond

Slander is making false oral statements about another person to a third party. It can lead to defamation which harms another's reputation, job with potential financial loss, and standing in the community. Do not gossip or whisper any rumours about your ex. Be careful whom you confide in during your divorce and what you reveal to them.

Libel is stating false allegations in writing and includes oral statements made through the media, such as a radio interview. Do NOT post anything about your divorce situation, or make any comments whatsoever about your spouse/ex on Facebook, Twitter or any other social media sites. Even if the information is true, it can be a lawsuit if they lose their job or volunteer position. Ask your attorney specific questions so that you do not jeopardize your divorce proceedings. Do not let a friend take any compromising photos of you, or post them on a social media site, particularly if you are holding a drink. You want to be viewed as a responsible person and not as a party girl or drunk, especially during a custody evaluation. Do not let anyone take nude photos of you at all in a future relationship. Leaks happen and celebrities have to deal with their sex videos being viewed online by millions. Learn from these mistakes.

Keep in mind that your privacy settings on social media sites may be strict, however, your friends may have lax ones that are easy to access by anyone, including your spouse's attorney. What you put on your sites for a few people to view, may show up on other people's Facebook. Several people have made the news due to getting fired for nasty remarks made about their bosses and companies on social media. Save your vitriol for in-person gossip sessions instead of airing it online. Make an oath that whatever is said does not leave the room.

One married father posted that he was single without kids on Match.Com. A single friend discovered this during his divorce and printed a copy for the wife. She gave copies to her attorney, Interim Child Psychologist, sons' therapist, and the Custody Evaluator. This was a costly mistake for that father and most likely affected the shared custody time.

What to do if you find out you are the target of lies on your ex's social media sites? Have a copy made of the remarks and others' comments on them. Save them in case they become more menacing or show a pattern of threats. I do not visit my ex's sites, but occasionally hear about his content from others. A few friends have either made copies or e-mailed me worrying remarks. I have a small file, just in case I need to have an attorney deal with them at a later point. Being the subject on your former partner's social media sites indicates that he/she is the one stuck in a holding pattern, not you. It is okay to be smug that you have moved on.

8

Alimony vs. Child Support

Alimony (maintenance) is taxable income for you, and child support is not taxed. Your ex gets a tax break with alimony, but does not get any with child support. Several women with young children chose to forgo alimony completely and only get child support, since they would be receiving it for over a decade. They did not have to pay any taxes on this income, which they would have had to do with alimony. What they did not pay in taxes was used to help pay off their mortgages and get them on their financial feet post-divorce. Since my sons were in middle and high school respectively, my attorney had me get more in alimony, because it would extend past my child support payments.

In some cases, women have opted not to receive any child support or alimony. Betty was pregnant at the time she was escaping from an abusive marriage. She chose not to tell her husband about the pregnancy, so she could cut marital ties quickly. She let him have most of the small stuff, and they expeditiously divided the main assets. Betty felt that her in-laws were toxic people, and did not wish them around her child. Soon afterward, she met a fabulous man, who has become one of the best dads on the planet to her son. Betty has not revealed whether or not her son even knows about his biological father.

Ramona was engaged to a man whom she thought had had a drug addiction in the distant past. When he fell into the abyss of addiction again, she discovered that she was pregnant and decided to leave. She also did not tell the future father, and so chose to receive no support. Now engaged to a kind man who loves this young boy, Ramona feels that she did the right thing. Ramona also has a large family with many positive male role models.

Katrina was married to a cruel man whom she divorced when their son was a baby. Katrina refused any type of support so that her husband would not have a financial interest vested in the child. Their son has very sporadic visits with his father. These are extreme situations where the women were satisfied with the choices they made, although not everyone else would agree. These decisions can be extremely difficult to make, but the situations leading to the unusual outcomes may be the best for all of the parties concerned.

States base alimony on how long you have been married. In my particular state, being married twenty years seems to be the magic number for a larger alimony. There is a formula which incorporates time married, how many children, the time spent at the parent's house who is receiving child support (such as 50/50), plus the amount of both people's wages. This is how the amount of child support/alimony is calculated in my region of the USA. My attorney stipulated that my alimony continues until the specified ending date, with no pre-payment. Have it put in the decree that you continue to receive alimony whether or not you remarry or cohabitate. Occasionally, people take the settlement in one huge, lump sum, as some celebrities opt to do, rather than in monthly payments. This is particularly good if you feel that your ex would disappear, or somehow would not have the money or make the payments down the road. You could invest the money yourself, which then could provide you with a monthly income.

There is modifiable and non-modifiable alimony, with pros and cons to both.

Non-modifiable is written in stone and cannot be changed at a later date. Modifiable can be altered if either parent's circumstances change after divorce. This requires going back to court or a mediator if unable to agree on it.

My husband wanted to revisit the alimony issue two years after our divorce, and the last thing I wanted to do was to go through the whole thing again. I went the non-modifiable route, with no changes allowed in the amount of my alimony, except if he declared bankruptcy. If your ex's income takes a nose dive post-divorce, but he does not declare bankruptcy, he is still responsible for the same amount of alimony. However, if it looks like he will be getting a prestigious promotion, or is starting to become a well-known author, you may want modifiable, so you can take him to court for an increase in alimony and child support. In cases where the woman out-earns the man, or if he was a stay-at-home father, then she may be ordered to pay alimony.

The new global trend is for the ex-spouse to pay a higher amount of alimony, for a shorter time period, usually for three to six years. This is Limited Duration Alimony. Many countries are moving away from alimony for life, even in long-term marriages where the wife never worked outside of the home. Spouses are expected to get training and be able to support themselves after alimony ceases.

I opted for this and used it to pay off my mortgage. I saved money by not paying my previous average of $1,700 per year in mortgage interest. I have two sons in college, so the extra amount of alimony is handy now. I usually put part of what I would have paid in mortgage payments into an investment account, so I will have a little nest egg when my alimony ends. The down side to this alimony arrangement is that the safety net is gone – no more divorce income for life. With this method, you really have to be disciplined and sock some money away for later years.

States have different calculations for the amount and duration for spousal support. These are online along with The American Academy of Matrimonial Lawyers' (AAML) recommendations. There were more variables in calculating alimony than with child support. States' results varied greatly for the duration of alimony with the same mythical information for children and salary. In Kansas it was 6.7 years, Maine 9.5 and Texas 5 years. There are factors for calculating the amount, such as what the current job market is like, so it is often determined by the financial advisor. The UK has many variables for calculating alimony and may be harder to predict the possible outcome.

I highly recommend that you have the alimony/support check automatically deposited into your bank account through your former spouse's financial institution. I cannot emphasize enough all the problems down the road that this protocol will prevent. Make sure that that this is actually put into your divorce decree. No "the check must have gotten lost in the mail" or having to contact your ex, to see why a check is late. Your ex is physically not involved with your monthly check; the two financial institutions are instead. Much easier.

Another way to do this is by garnishing the payer's wages for the amount of alimony/child support. The payer must have an employer and not be self-employed. The employer takes the payment out of the wages after receiving papers from the court.

Calculating Child Support

Each state, the UK and many other countries have online calculators that one can easily use to figure out approximately what child support would be. I took two mythical children over age twelve with the same amount of overnights, and parental income to ascertain child support. In North Carolina it would be $847/month and in another state it was $1271.00. The same calculations for England resulted in $799.00 per month. If you have the option of filing for divorce in two states or countries, you may want to do these calculations first to get an idea of what to expect in each one. In some states child support is based upon both parents' income and in others only on the noncustodial parent's income.

In the UK, as is a similar one in the U.S., there is Child Maintenance Service (CMC). This acts as an intermediary between parents to collect child support (maintenance). Sometimes a small fee is charged for this service. They keep track of payments and can go after deadbeat parents who are late, or not paying the required support. This can save on legal fees if non-payment becomes a chronic problem. About once a year the CMC reviews the income records supplied by Her Majesty's Revenue & Customs (HMRC), to see if there is a change in the payer's income. If there is, then maintenance is automatically adjusted (supersession).The CMC will give the parents twenty-eight days' notice before a change is made. They have fourteen days to reply. If there is no answer, or the reply is in agreement, then the change occurs. If the payer's income increases by at least 25%, then an appeal may be submitted to get an increase in maintenance before this yearly evaluation. If the payer knows that there will be a drastic change in his financial circumstance, such as a job loss, then he can apply ahead of time to reduce the maintenance that he will have to pay.

In many places including the UK, there is a guide for the percentage of child support to be taken from a father's salary. For example, if a man makes over £100 per week and has three or more children, then 31% could be deducted from his pay check. Since this is for three or more children, it is the same amount deducted even if there are ten children. It does not matter how many mothers are involved. They would split the 31% depending upon how many children each had with this father.

In England another factor into child support is how many other children are living with the father, such as step-children. If the father has two biological children and he makes over £100/week, then 25% could be the amount he owes in child support. However, if he has one step-child, the percentage goes down to 21.2%. With two step-children, then 19.9%, and with three step-children he would only pay 18.9% to his biological children's mother for their support.

9

Dividing Assets

Factor in future interest payments when dividing up assets. For example, if your spouse gets $200,000 cash or assets up front and you opt to wait until something sells to get yours, then you have lost potential interest. If your spouse will give you a $200,000 piece of property in a year's time, the annual interest @ 3% is $6,000. That is $6,000 you would lose in delaying the receipt of this asset, so that has to be factored into the division when settling. You would have to get something else to compensate for the loss of the $6,000 or receive the asset promptly.

While the divorce financial adviser will do an impartial job valuing assets and determining how much each spouse receives, it is up to you to decide what particular assets you want. It is prudent to diversify them. For example, if you want the $200,000 house, you will have to give up $100,000 in assets to your spouse. If your partner chooses to receive their half from a money market account, and the housing market crashes, your half of the value of the house could be a lot less than $100,000. If, in a year, the value of the house decreases to $140,000, your share is really only $70,000.

Sometimes it may be better to sell the house, pay off the mortgage and split the difference. Keep in mind a $100,000 pension plan is not the same as a $100,000 house. A pension plan or money market accrues interest and increases in value, while a house requires funds for upkeep, taxes, and insurance. There is no guarantee that a house will appreciate in value. Consider consulting with a real estate agent to discuss projected housing market trends in your area. You will gain insight whether or not the house is a good investment. Meeting with your own financial advisor can determine if it is feasible to take on the house with a mortgage. The financial advisor can also look over the assets in general, and see which would be more advantageous in your particular circumstance.

When children and pets are residing in the house it may be worthwhile to stay put. If you move, your children may belong in another school district and be unable to transfer into their current school the following year. There may not be other properties in your school district to rent or purchase. Moving across town can impact their friendships and activities. If you have great neighbours and like the shops and cafes in your locale, this is another reason to remain in the marital home.

Life coaches excel in helping people who are stuck on an issue to see the pros and cons of various decisions. They can help clarify a situation and help one to make the best choice whether to stay or sell the marital home. Ask others who have trod down the path of divorce, for their input in on selling or buying your spouse out of the property. Talking out this situation with others can help you to see potential pitfalls or having it be the right decision.

Other options to do when keeping the house, are to get a roommate or have a home-based business, if possible. There is a tax-break for a home-based business, when having your office there to see clients. Part of the mortgage and utilities are a deduction. Several therapists that I know of have converted their garages into client therapy rooms. You can list a bedroom as a holiday rental on sites such as Airbnb. Then you control when you want a tourist to stay with you and when you need that bedroom for family. One mother rents out her daughter's room when she is at college to help pay for her tuition and gives the student a bit of spending money. Spareroom.co.uk is about having a lodger during the work week who vacates your premises on the weekends. One can earn £4250 in rent per year tax free in the UK.

My acquaintance Hazel, was in a rocky marriage with divorce as a probable outcome. They sometimes vacationed in Prescott, Arizona and she decided to retire there. She persuaded her spouse that they should buy a vacation home in Prescott, and Hazel selected a gem. During their divorce proceedings in New England, her husband was happy to give her the small vacation home. Both houses had no mortgages, so Hazel ended up with some cash as an equalization. Hazel advises other women to plan ahead, especially if unsure about their marriages.

There are various tax consequences for assets. Some fall under capital gains and others may be taxed at a higher rate in one's income tax bracket. Still others may be tax deferred which is paid after retirement or not at all. Consider what taxes have to be paid now or at a later date when selecting assets. Two $100K assets can actually be worth different amounts, after the taxes owed on them are assessed. In England for example, a £50,000 investment could owe capital gains tax, yet owe nothing if put into an ISA account. See if assets can be rolled over into plans where little or no tax will be owed. Investment bonds have a tax liability if cashed. If they are assigned to the person in the lower tax bracket, then the divorcing spouses are keeping more of their wealth. In high net worth divorces, having a tax specialist working along with the financial advisor can be beneficial in the division of assets. If you are divorcing in November or December, then you will sign the divorce papers, but it will not be filed with the court until January 2nd. Otherwise, you would be filing two tax returns for the same year, one married and one single. On January 2nd, you start off the tax year as single.

Clean Break is a new way of dividing assets that is particularly done in Scotland. The assets are divided and that is it, except for child support. If one spouse needs some money for training or to finish a degree, then extra may be awarded in the Clean Break, as it would be in other divorces. This is to get away from one spouse paying alimony to the other one. In The States, some couples usually without children, may do this. My friend was quite happy to have a Clean Break from her spouse and just split their few assets without future support in their divorce.

If your husband applied for a patent or wrote a book while still married, then you have negotiating rights for future payments. If you worked and helped put your husband through grad school, then see if you can get more future earnings or some type of payback. A few women have taken a small percentage of their professional spouse's income for a set number of years as payment for supporting him through medical or law school.

Make sure your lawyer and financial adviser are aware of other perks, such as their frequent flier miles, or hotel points, which could be divided or traded for other assets. If he/she wants to keep your joint country club or golf membership, check what its value is now. Call the country club yourself and talk with the membership department to find out what it is worth or what it would cost to buy it at this moment.

Pension Plan Division

You may be entitled to part of your spouse's employer sponsored pension plans, such as a 401(k). It may be that one party gets the pension plan and the other one gets a major asset, such as the marital home. If the plan is divided then a Qualified Domestic Relations Order (QDRO) is put into place, which is a court order. The QDRO are specific instructions that spells out for the plan administer exactly how the plan is to be divided between spouses. This type of pension plan is covered under the Employer Retirement Income Security Act (ERISA). There are different aspects to choosing to division of a pension plan and the specifics of how to do so. Some pension plan payments stop when the person dies without a survivor benefit. The ex-spouse may not receive much if the death occurs right after retirement.

Various ways to handle a QDRO are to form a separate account for the spouse (alternate payee) within the plan. Another way is for a direct rollover with the funds designated to the alternate payee into an approved pension, such as an IRA. Check on the minimum age (such as sixty) for this to avoid a penalty. The last method is for the plan administrator to send a check to the alternative payee for the amount awarded in the QDRO. There may be a tax consequence for this, but at least the money is received when there is not a survivor benefit.

Some considerations to think about is that a pension plan gains interest and value. A house may appreciate, but requires cash for taxes, insurance and maintenance. A $200,000 dollar house and pension plan are not equal assets due to the house's ongoing expenses. Also, a $200,000 money market account and pension plan may not be equal if taxes have to be paid on the distribution received from a pension plan and the other accrues interest. Have a financial advisor check the tax liability on a Roth vs a Traditional IRA for accurate division. You may want your own financial advisor to study pensions and other assets that are to be divided, to determine what is advantageous for you. The important message is to be aware of any taxes that have to be paid down the road for assets in order to make division more equitable.

One woman was thrilled when her ex-husband retired and she started receiving his pension payments. She blew it on items for her house and did not save any of it. Her former spouse died soon afterwards. Her sister asked if she had informed the pension plan administer of his untimely death. She had not and refused to believe that these payments would stop with his demise. Well, she had a shock when the administrator forced her to return the few payments received after her ex's death. Paying the tax penalty on option three for a bulk sum would have been more beneficial in this woman's case.

If you are to receive half of your spouse's retirement plan, consider stipulating the percentage (50%), rather than inserting an actual monetary amount in case it becomes larger with accrued interest. In one case, Jane received half of her husband's $100,000 retirement plan in her divorce. The number $50,000 was stipulated as the amount she would receive upon her husband's retirement a decade later. New York State had a large increase to retirement accounts and instead of $100K, the pension jumped to $130,000. Joan received the $50,000 instead of half, which would have been $65,000.

Parental Assistance and Gifts Pre-Divorce

If your parents paid a credit card bill for your husband, as my mother did, find that record. She was able to get her $6,800 back in the divorce, because she had the cancelled check showing that she directly paid his MasterCard bill one month. If your parents loaned you both some money, make sure they are paid back first, before assets are divided.

This is particularly important if your parents helped you with a down payment or helped with any principle or mortgage payments. Get documentation. Elena's mother helped a couple buy their first house, so her name was also on the deed. This was tremendous help in her daughter's divorce. The bank had changed hands and the financial officer had retired, so they did not have good documentation for the mother's share of the house. The lawyers were going to give the couple and the wife's mother each a one third share of the house. By chance, the wife ran into the retired bank financial officer during the divorce and quickly called her lawyer's paralegal from the grocery store and got this woman on the phone. So, instead of buying her husband out for a one third share, it was now only one sixth. Any records from your parents can assist in divvying up assets when they have contributed some of the payments.

If any big ticket items were a personal gift to you from your parents, have them put that in writing to your attorney. My mother had to do this, so some furniture and other items were not counted as joint assets in my divorce. This would be particularly important in the case of a car or an expensive piece of artwork given as a gift to you personally from your family. Unfortunately, if money or stock gifts received from your family were merged into a joint account, then it is joint property in a divorce.

Credit Cards

During your divorce, joint accounts and credit cards may be closed. Each spouse would then have a credit card in his or her name to prevent future liability issues. The balance on our two credit cards was completely paid off before we received any assets. Post-divorce, we each started with a clean slate.

Ask to claim the children as dependents on your tax form. My attorney calculated that my husband would only save about $35 per child, due to his higher tax bracket. However, if I claimed the boys, I would save a few hundred dollars each, because of my much lower one. My husband's lawyer readily agreed that it made more sense for me to take this deduction post-divorce.

Differences between Equity and Community Property States

Most states have the equity system which is based on English Common Law. As in the UK today – a couple's total situation is taken into consideration – not just the value of the assets themselves. If a person gave up her job to raise kids and be supportive of her high earning spouse's career, then that is a factor in asset division. A spouse out of the job market for years, or in a low paying job may get a little more of the goods as compensation for less potential earning post-divorce. Equity states look to see what is fair to both spouses.

Marital property is that which is jointly owned by a couple, such as the house they bought after marriage. Non-marital property is what was received as gifts, or an inheritance that was not co-mingled. When a personal asset is put into a joint account, or a spouse's name added to it, that is considered co-mingled and subject to being split in divorce.

Community property states base their system on Spanish and Mexican law. The husband and wife each own half of the assets and income derived from them. This community property is divided up equally between spouses. The individual assets, such as a pension plan are not split 50/50, but rather the total value of all is divided in half. Various assets may be assigned to either person as a whole or some, such as a bank account, may be split in half.

Separate property is the name for non-marital property in community property states. It includes what each party brought into the marriage. The Traceable Rule tracks how and when the property or asset was acquired to determine if it is separate or community property. A Tort award or worker's comp is not divided when it was granted to pay medical expenses for a personal injury. If these are for income replacement – then that portion would be assessed for as being possible community property.

An Equitable Lien is when community property (money) is used to maintain or add value to a separate property. If the husband owned a horse ranch before marriage and community property funds were utilized to enlarge and upgrade it, that is an Equitable Lien. While the husband would retain ownership of it post-divorce, the wife could receive a portion of the funds used for its improvements. It is the money spent and not any labour that may be reimbursed in a divorce settlement. If she mucked out the stalls, that labour is not repaid.

A divorcing spouse may receive a reimbursement of community property spent on a third party during marriage. This is a fictional example. Alfred bought his mistress Lola a $200K condo during his marriage with community funds. Alfred's wife, Alice wonders why there seems to be a discrepancy with their bank account and meets with the bank manager. Alice files for divorce after discovering the existence of Lola and the condo. Alice is entitled to get back ½ of the community funds ($100,000) that was used to purchase it. Even though the condo has appreciated to $250K, the original purchase price is used for the calculation, not appreciation or depreciation amounts.

Couples are increasing purchasing second homes to stay in closer contact with far flung family members. There are considerations to be made when splitting assets in both equity and community property states. If they live in New York (equity) and purchased a second home in Arizona (community property), the laws of New York would prevail for the division of property. If they lived in Arizona and bought a condo in NYC, it would be just the opposite. If one spouse files for divorce in California and the other in Ohio, the two courts would decide which state has the most contact with the parties and has jurisdiction. The 1040 tax form may be checked to verify primary residence.

Post-Divorce Tasks

Check the title of your car to ensure that you are the sole owner. Make sure to remove your former spouse's name from assets that you received in your divorce, including bank or money market accounts. You may be required to show your divorce decree stating what you received in your divorce. Make sure any retirement plans and other investments also have been changed to your name only. Verify any loans that were assigned solely to your former spouse, do not include your name on them. You do not want creditors trying to extract money from you at a future date for these loans.

If you got the marital house in the divorce, take your spouse's name off the deed and amend the record with your state or country, for future taxes. Ensure that your name is removed from any loans assigned to the other party post-divorce.

Estate Planning Post-Divorce

Post-divorce, protect your assets by drawing up a new will. Remove your ex-spouse as a beneficiary and have the assets instead go to your children, your siblings and other people. I have read about irate second wives receiving much less, because their late husbands forgot to remove the former wife's name from various financial investments as a beneficiary. These men merely added their new wives' names as an addition.

Also, name a guardian for underage children if your former spouse is abusive or has limited contact with the children. This helps to prevent the other parent from automatically receiving guardianship. The situation is formally investigated when another guardian has been appointed by the custodial parent in their will. In one case, the two sons said that they would run away if their mother died and their father was granted custody. One even interviewed homeless people and got input which area was the safest. Select, as executor of your will, the person best able to carry out your wishes. If you leave your assets to children who are minors, naming a guardian also can prevent your ex from managing these funds.

Please include a provision for any pets, so that they will have a home and some funds for maintenance. I recently took care of a cat who had been a loving companion to an elderly lady. When she died, her adult offspring kicked the sweet cat out onto the street. Luckily, this kitty was found

by a kind-hearted person, who brought her to our cat rescue
organization.

10

Dividing Personal Property

Pick your battles because haggling over every little thing increases legal fees and can prolong the divorce. My attorney said that couples have split millions of dollars in assets calmly, but divorces have nearly derailed while trying to divide personal property. This subject is a minefield, so my attorney does it at the very end of the divorce process. Unfortunately, my sons and I had to move out of the family house, because it had to be renovated for resale during our divorce, so we had to deal with this issue earlier than we would have preferred.

Methods of Division

There are different ways to approach this, but often the spouse still in the house often does the household inventory. Items may be listed with a value, after the more expensive ones are professionally appraised. Other times, just the items are listed without any values and the spouses each take similar items in the different categories. You might each take an antique, or similar household furnishings. If you are not sure what particular artwork to request, consider hiring your own art appraiser to give you some guidance.

Other spouses each have one colour of stickers and take turns putting them on desired objects. They flip a coin to see who goes first. There is give and take with this process.

Some attorneys have their clients make three separate lists: What you really want, what you would like and what you do not particularly care about. If your spouse is spiteful, this can be the most trying and tedious part of the whole divorce.

Personal property, such a jewellery is usually exempt from the asset division. This may seem unfair if one party has valuable gems and the other one a few pins or rings. I have sterling silver jewellery and my former husband, 18K gold. It was not worth battling over the inequality which would only bog down the proceedings.

Lump your spouse's gifts and heirlooms from relatives and friends (including wedding presents) in one category, and do the same for you. You each would get your category as personal property. Some individuals already removed valuable and sentimental heirlooms from their homes during their turbulent marriages and gave them to a family member to store for safekeeping. Any furniture, art or personal effects that we each brought into the marriage remained ours in the personal property division. I clearly put this on the household inventory and marked the appropriate name by it. This was not up for negotiation.

The sheriff's department will send a deputy to be present, while your spouse removes their allowed items, if notified ahead of time. A better option for me was to have my attorney's paralegal present the entire time that my husband packed up and moved his designated goods out of our house. She had a list of the inventory and kept him on track. I did not have to worry that something not on his list would be taken either on purpose or by accident.

I stored my older clothes and other personal items in my mother's garage during my divorce. I waited until after the divorce to take them to charity shops so I could claim the tax-write off on my next year's tax form. If you take items to charity shops during your divorce, then you split the tax write-off on your last married tax form that is filed with your spouse.

A regret that Kelly has is that she did not take much personal property when leaving with her two children. She left most of their toys, clothes and her own artwork (she's a painter) behind. Since Kelly took the kids across the state line erroneously, she lost her bargaining power and gave up most of her personal property in order to avoid more legal entanglements. A parent is not allowed to take a child across the state line without permission from or notification to the other parent. This is to prevent parental kidnapping or moving across country with the kids.

If you have a friendly relationship with your spouse, maybe just the two of you can get their stuff packed and out of the house. A few times, when my husband wanted this or that, I would leave it on the front porch at a designated time for pick up. This arrangement was done through my attorney.

A few couples I know felt that the division of personal property was taking up too much time with lawyers (more expensive). They met at coffee houses and got the inventory done and the division agreed upon during one or two meetings. The cappuccinos added a friendlier touch.

In some instances one spouse is vindictive and tries to mete out punishment through asset division. In Mia's case, her husband felt that he deserved the bulk of it and tried to stake his claim. Mia said it takes two to dance and decided to sit that one out. There were just a few absolutely must haves and she told her husband to "take the rest." "The rest" lost its appeal when Max saw that Mia was not going to get upset and march into battle. Mia then got more than she had anticipated. Mia and Max had owned a business together before the divorce and there was artwork, handmade furniture, and other items in that establishment that had been purchased with joint marital funds. The financial advisor pointed out that Mia would get a portion of these besides the household ones. Since Max wanted to maintain the exact appearance of the business, he became amenable to letting Mia have the majority of household assets in lieu of business ones. Max still had to extract revenge, so left some personal gifts behind from Mia and the children. She had the last laugh when she netted several hundred dollars from them on E-bay and a used book store. The tax-write off for others post-divorce was nice.

Pets may be divided up like personal property, with whomever you brought into the marriage remaining with you. Our cats have close ties with each other and particular friendships within the group. My feline-loving attorney stated that the cats needed to stay together as a unit. No one said anything and I held my breath, since I was the one who always took care of them. My attorney announced that they would remain with me and quickly moved on to the next topic. In a few cases the dog goes with the children when they have visitation with each parent. Be creative. Sometimes animal custody can be the main sticky point with a divorce.

When Benny and Barb parted ways they had to decide who got custody of their dog. Since Barb had a house it made more sense for her to keep the hound. Benny is on good terms with his ex and house sits when she and her partner go on vacation. Benny is happy to spend time with his former dog and this situation benefits everyone. He also housesits for a few other friends to get his "dog fix."

Take the high road in divorce. Do not be like the couple in the 1989 movie, "War of the Roses" (Kathleen Turner and Michael Douglas) who did not take the high road and fought to the bitter end. Nobody won and the results were deadly. It is better to get through a divorce with one's sanity intact than to get into a knock-out battle. Two of my friends wanted out of their marriages and left with few community possessions. They both said that china and other goods were not worth the time and emotional burden it would take if they fought over them. Consequently, their divorces were both quick, and these people got nice china, artwork and houses in their subsequent marriages. Plus, the new pieces did not carry the memories of the last relationship. Several well-known people have used this quote, "I'm going to take the High Road because the Low Road is so crowded."

11

Family Members during Divorce

Parenting during Divorce

Remember that you are a parent and not a good buddy. Continue to enforce boundaries and rules. It is important to establish a new bond with your children during divorce, since they may have viewed you as part of a unit. Jacqueline Kennedy stated, "If you bungle raising your children, I don't think whatever else you do well matters very much."

Reassure children that you will receive interim support during the divorce. Give the kids some control in this unsettling situation. Ask, "How can we cut our spending?" When children are involved in solutions, they are happier complying with new financial strategies. You would be surprised at how creative little ones can be. Look on the ground for money. We seem to find enough for ice cream treats. Eat out for breakfast instead of dinner. Use public transportation. Have a pizza night at home and rent or borrow a DVD from the library. Papa Murphy's has fresh, made-to-order pizzas that you pick up and bake later. Take a picnic lunch by a river or to a lovely park.

Other people have called the Chamber of Commerce, or have gone online to discover what free events and festivals are happening in their communities. Have potluck suppers with other single moms and kids. I often meet my friends at coffee shops, split a pastry and catch up with gossip. It is a lot cheaper than a full meal.

If your family asks what to get you and the kids for Christmas, suggest that they pool their gifts into one and buy a gift card to an amusement park. At my local grocery store, there are three day passes to Disneyland and that would be a fabulous way to forget about the divorce for a few days. There also are affordable weekend getaway packages that would be a great group present.

Teenagers

Communicating with teenagers can be challenging in the best conditions, so here are a few tips to make this easier in divorce. Be direct and to the point when communicating with teenagers. When dining in front of the television, say "Feet," instead of a long tirade of "Even a first grader knows not to put his feet on the coffee table." Use one word or a short phrase to convey your message. Teens tune us out quickly.

Leave a short note, written in a bright colour of marker, taped to the bathroom mirror. For example, "Take out the trash" written in neon green will grab his attention.

When they are required to do a task, get a firm time commitment. If the response is, "Yeah, I'll do it later," ask what time the task will be completed, so you do not keep nagging. If he says "eight o'clock," then do not give time reminders, such as "It is fifteen minutes until eight." After the first time or two, the teen gets the job done in a timely manner, knowing you will not keep harping about it.

Ask your teen to take a walk with you, and often this will be the time where he opens up about what is on his mind. I go to the restaurant where my sons work. It is lovely to be waited on by a young man (son) who gives attentive service and asks about my day.

Just hang out with your son and do parallel activities together. He may be playing a video game while you are reading your favourite magazine. Being together in the same room is still quality time, even if not having a conversation.

Adult Offspring

Adult offspring may feel grief at losing their childhood home and the other changes taking place. They may need space from both parents to work through these swirling emotions. Talk with them about what they are experiencing, how they are feeling about it, and what they need to help them feel better. Acknowledge their angry or sad feelings. These young adults do not require an in depth analysis of what went wrong in your marriage. Even if the other parent had an affair, do not put down the other parent.

Adult offspring may feel as much adrift as younger ones. They may be married and have their own children, yet feel caught in your tug of war. Do not try to sway them to your side or to choose a parent over the other one. Do not expect them to be your confidantes; call your friends instead. Do not ask them to be witnesses in litigation, as my stepmother did to me. (I turned down this request). Counselling can be a beneficial tool for children of all ages.

Pets

Remember that your pets feel emotions and can pick up on the anxieties and anger in their environment. Cats and dogs may be facing a change in residence as part of your divorce. They do not understand what is happening, so they may require more TLC and attention. Taking your dog on extra walks will increase your exercise, thus improving your health and well-being. Various studies have indicated that one can lower their blood pressure and calm the nervous system when petting cats. Their purr induces relaxation. Having cats that wanted to be on my lap, forced me to relax, put my feet up, and read a magazine. I needed this break in the midst of chaos. Enlist the kids to provide some additional playtime for Rover and Tigger.

Many veterinarians recommend Bach's Rescue Remedy for animals, especially those who stress out when going to the clinic. If your pets are moving into a new environment due to the divorce, check with your veterinarian to see if Rescue Remedy is right for them. There are other brands of homeopathic sprays that also help to calm animals. Our cat rescue group uses Feliway, a plug-in diffuser that releases cat pheromones to calm the cats. My veterinarian also recommends this product for cats during stressful situations such as divorce, to reassure them and lessen any maladaptive behaviours.

Stepmothers in Divorce

Staying in contact with young step-children is more challenging than when they are older. When my stepmother divorced my father, I was in college, so it was very easy to maintain contact with her and the extended family. Since I could drive, I popped in and continued to enjoy family activities. My step-grandparents, aunts, uncles and cousins treated me in the same loving way post-divorce.

When my father died, I was not able to attend the funeral home viewing, but I did attend the funeral. My mother and stepmother went to the viewing together. My mother gleefully proclaimed to his former co-workers and friends that they were "members of the former wives club."

If you have young step-children and are divorcing, be sure to address visitations as part of your divorce decree. If your former husband is going to have them every other week, then maybe you could see them for part of a day on one of those visits. If you have an amicable relationship with their biological mother, then offer give their mum a break and enjoy some time with the kids. Reassure the children that you are their friend and want to continue being a part of their lives. Make sure that they have your contact information.

Saying No to Hosting Family or Other Guests

If you are the one who usually hosts holiday dinners, and this is too daunting during divorce, be honest about it. Inquire how holiday family get-togethers can be tweaked. Perhaps a sibling would do the event if it were a brunch instead of a dinner. This is the time to bring up rotating family holiday events, with your name at the bottom of the list. Many families do pot-luck, with the host mainly supplying the home, dishes and utensils. Another option is to meet at a restaurant which is festive and reasonable. After my mother's divorce, we ate Thanksgiving dinners at a nearby restaurant that served lovely meals family style. Another divorced mother and her daughter met us there.

When married, you may have hosted a barrage of guests at your seaside cottage or mountain retreat. It can be hard to say "no" when they are accustomed to staying at your house regularly. What has worked for some folks is telling acquaintances that it is great they will be in their locale, and to please save a night or two for a get-together. Others give a time limit up front, such as three days due to court hearings and so forth. You can ask potential guests if they need a bus schedule or information on car rentals, since you will be working. People forget that the hosts still have to go to work and may not want to use up valuable vacation time. It may be easier to be more direct with family members, stating that you cannot handle houseguests during this turbulent time.

Some people have let the guests themselves decide that they really do not want to stay at their houses. One woman felt that her kids should take precedence over adult's activities at Christmas. Her aunt was self-centred and had been wined and dined during the woman's marriage. She told this relative that she was welcome to stay over Christmas as usual, but from now on the focus would be on the children. They would be watching family holiday specials on television, baking cookies, and hanging out near the decorated tree. The aunt decided on her own to avoid this child-centred Christmas, and has found somewhere else that she needed to be at that time of year ever since.

12

Visitation

Problem: How shared time can be smoother for the children

Solution: Unless you have an amicable divorce situation, have a neutral drop off and return place. I chose an assigned drop-off place, as it was too stressful for my sons and me to have their father drop them off at my house. I did not want him around my property. The boys tended to fly out of his car before it even stopped. Some parents have been late with pick-ups and drop-offs, and the kids have had to wait by a window, watching for their car. This can impact your plans, especially if you are meeting people for a show. If this happens, ask them to call you beforehand, if they're running late, so you have the option of making a new arrangement. After the second time they are late for a pick-up, or if the kids are returned late, contact your attorney to have visitation enforced or modified.

• If the drop-off place for older children is a public place, such as a coffee shop, then their other parent is more likely to pick them up on time to avoid public embarrassment. A day-care or preschool can be a drop off and pick up point for young kids, and is easier when both parents have car seats. A neutral drop off place is better in an acrimonious divorce, and then children do not witness angry parents attempting to interact.

• During and also post-divorce, treat any interaction with your co-parent as if it were a business situation. State facts and keep your emotions out of it.

• Children do not want to feel like visitors, especially when joining new step-siblings, so have them unpack right away. No one cares to live out of a suitcase, so give the kids their own space. A drawer or large bin is fine, if these are dedicated only to them.

• Taking a few objects back and forth between visitations helped my sons. One took a small stone in his pocket and touched its smooth surface to calm himself. The younger one brought a small toy that he could take out of his pocket when anything overwhelmed him. Youngsters may want a stuffed animal friend who is always with them. What helps is to have the same checklist at each house to make sure that these items come back each time with the children. As a nurse, I saw the same child several times with stomach aches and it turned out that he kept leaving a necessary book at one's parent's house during visitation. A few others were distressed that they left homework and school reports at the other parent's home. Have a bright neon coloured folder containing school work that travels between homes and is on the mutual checklist.

• Consider letting children take gifts back and forth, particularly when they are small in size. One parent "gave" an Xbox to his teenage son as his only birthday present. The son was disappointed when the gift had to stay at that parent's house, although the teen was encouraged "to come over any time" that he wanted to play with it. He did not have a car and due to previous abuse, had very limited visitation. A present must be given freely, without strings attached. If a parent wants a gaming device, then buy it and consider purchasing some special games for the teen to enjoy during visitation.

• Using Skype is an option for children to stay in touch with the other parent during visitation. This is especially good when one parent travels a lot or lives in a different locale. Connecting with the absent parent is reassuring to the child and maintains the parental bond. Some psychologists recommend having children call the other parent during visitations. My sons' time with their father was short, so this was unnecessary for us. My parents got divorced when I was four and I would have felt awkward calling the other parent. Perhaps allow a young child to call when he misses the other one. Keeping in contact depends upon the child and what seems best in his particular situation. There is a balance between staying in touch and being intrusive of the other parent during visitation times. I reassured my sons that I would be having lattes with girlfriends during their visitation so that they did not worry about me.

• Do not ask how visitation went or what your son and the other parent did. Your child may not want to admit that he had a fun day at the amusement park in order to spare your feelings, especially if it looks like you have been crying.

• In some cases, the nanny goes back and forth to both homes with the children. She then ensures consistent routines and gives stressed-out parents a break.

Visitation Transitions

Problem: How can visitation transitions be made easier?

Solution: The most challenging time can be the transitions of moving back and forth between parents, especially for younger children. They are settled in and now it is time to go back to the other place. Very young children are already dealing with separation anxiety, so you must present a positive demeanour with this transition. Each parent's attitude sets the tone for the exchange, so at least be matter of fact. Some mothers at my sons' preschool were on the verge of tears when parting, which is not therapeutic at all.

• Consider having a goodbye ritual to enable the child to ease into this transition. There may be a special story that is read or a song that is sung while packing. The child may draw a picture that is given to the other parent upon greeting them. My sons had a goodbye routine with our cats.

• Some parents have a welcome back routine when their children return after being with the other parent. This gives the kids something to anticipate upon arrival. My step-mother had pizza night and we watched fun TV shows or a movie. Dad sometimes may take the youngsters to Gran's for a yummy dinner, or Mum might have delicious homemade treats. The trick is to make the transitions more pleasant, making it easier for the child to enjoy time with each parent. Sometimes a child may want to chill out and regroup. Give him space and let him rejoin you a bit later.

• Chamomile tea or lavender facial mist are some measures to help the transfer to be more relaxing. If the transfers between parental homes are an issue, then consider having a session with a divorce coach or mediator. It may be that the transitions are too frequent and a better schedule with longer stays at each parent's home is advisable. Or one parent has the child for a longer stay and the other one picks the kid up for a day or takes her to a movie in the evening. A neutral third party can tweak a visitation schedule with too many transfers to benefit the child.

Taking Care of You during Visitation

Emma has these words of wisdom: "Alone is different from being lonely." The difference between the two is that she felt victimized when she was feeling lonely. Realization brought the concept that quiet time (being alone) is nice. During visitation, when her two sons were with their father, Emma learned that she could use that time for spiritual growth and meditation. Emma felt "poor me" at first, but has a different perspective now. Your "story" (past) takes root in childhood and influences the way you see the world and your particular situation. She felt that her divorce experience was much worse than it had to be due to not letting go of her "story." Emma had been adopted and her divorce triggered abandonment issues.

• The first several times of visitation will be especially difficult, so decide if you would rather be alone or be distracted by your pals. During the second visitation, I was in a small shop and just lost it. The sales clerk, bless her heart, acted like nothing was different and finished our transaction. I finally blurted out about visitation. She had already guessed that was the problem and proceeded to tell me of her experiences with her young tots. This young woman assured me that future visitations would get easier, and she was right.

• Be a tourist in your own hometown. Visit museums, the Botanical Garden and other special sites. Check out your city's event calendar and attend festivals, concerts and art fairs. Your single pals may like to join you in this fun. Married friends might enjoy doing something girly while the guys in their families are going dirt biking or camping. Your mates might want to join you at the pub while their wives are out shopping.

• Can you put in extra time at work during visitation and take more time off when you are with your children? There may be other single parents who would like flexibility and you trade coverage for each other.

• I went to foreign films, oldies, or the more avant-garde movies when my boys were away. I also used visitation time to get a pedicure. I took some non-credit cooking classes at our community college which only lasted several hours on the weekend.

• Volunteer during the kids' time away. One divorced mom did Meals-on-Wheels when without kids and had so many interesting stories to share.

13

Co-Parenting

Problem: How co-parenting can be more effective and less nerve-racking

Solution: Co-parenting can be easier as time marches on and heals wounds. Remember this is all about the children and not about scoring points or being in a popularity contest. Leave anger and judgments out of interactions with your ex. If he or she becomes agitated, suggest resuming the discussion when they are calm. Do not let the other parent trigger your hot buttons.

- Try to be on the same page with basic routines, such as meals and bedtimes. Children are clever and may try to manipulate you both into getting extra privileges. If you have a united front, than this is less problematic and you can both firmly state the common rules.
- Be flexible when the other parent's request is reasonable, such as having the kids a little extra time when his out-of-town relatives are visiting. Children will appreciate your generosity and could feel hurt if they missed a reunion. Do not say "no" out of vindictiveness, only if it is not in the children's best interest. If you feel that requests are getting out of hand or there is too much switching going on, then perhaps meeting with a mediator or counsellor may be in order. This is a reality check for you both, so that a better plan can be implemented.

• Children want both parents to attend school events and important milestones. If you can sit together for these, then great. If not, keep your emotions in check and remain polite, even if from across the auditorium. There will be important functions such as First Communions or Bar Mitzvahs that you both will want to attend. Even if he brings his new trophy wife who broke up your marriage, smile when you grit your teeth, because she is their step-mother. She may be very loving and kind to the kids. You do have class and model this dignity to your children. If you do not like your ex-wife's new partner, be polite anyways, for the sake of the kids.

• Of course, the other parent gave the kids half of their DNA, so never say anything mean about him or her. In my case, I find it better to say nothing whatsoever at all. Do not make children choose sides. If you can have a few friendly words on the doorstep or occasionally invite him or her in for coffee, the kids will appreciate this. Some former spouses get together on holidays with their children, for at least part of the day. You may have had an adversarial marital relationship, but that is now behind you. What lies ahead is being on the same team to ensure the children are safe, happy and thriving. During and post-divorce treat any interaction with their other parent as if it were a business situation. State facts and keep your emotions out of it. If co-parenting truly is unmanageable, then a mediator can step in to handle all communication between both of you.

• There are some web sites and apps that have an online calendar that both parents can access to add activities and events. This is a great way for parents to be on the same page and know about games, school activities, and fixed events. Communication can be challenging post-divorce and this calendar can reduce its frequency, plus is devoid of any emotion. Make sure that the school has both parents' contact information, including e-mail addresses, and sends duplicate reports and notices.

• Avoid competing with your ex, instead bring your warmth and unique qualities to your relationship with your kids. One parent may have wealth, however love and attention are far more important. Gadgets are superficial, but time spent with children is enduring. When co-parenting with a toxic ex, tell the kids "learn from both of our strengths and mistakes so that you can be great parents."

• Do not make excuses for the other parent if they miss visitations or do not follow through with promises. You do not know what is in the other parent's heart or mind. This may raise the child's hopes and expectations when in reality the other parent is attempting to fade from the picture. Instead focus on the child. Acknowledge his feelings of disappointment and frustration. Suggest a diversion, such as calling a chum for a sleepover or pizza and a movie.

• Avoid having the kids in the middle of a tug of war. Sharing too much divorce information or anxieties is detrimental to children. They do not want to be coerced into choosing sides. Avoid making ultimatums to your children. When I was 21, my father was quite annoyed that I stayed in contact with his former wife and family. He gave me the ultimatum that it was either him or them. I chose them.

• Realize that children may tell you what they think you want to hear. Or youngsters may tell you things about the other parent that are more in the fantasy realm. Take what the child says about the other parent "with a grain of salt." When I was around five, I would tell my father that my mother had a maid. It was purely wishful thinking.

Jessica was married to a physician who was busy and rarely around for her or the kids. They grew apart and got a divorce. Tracy married young and had the first of her two babies soon afterward. While she settled down to night feedings and doing the bulk of childcare, Cedric was out around town with his mates. Staying home was not on his radar. Jenny's husband Eddie was a big kid himself and full of fun. He'd say, "Don't let Mum catch us eating all of this candy" or ask the kids, "Do you want to work around the house or go to the park?" Another woman whose husband's excessive traveling led to their parting, was surprised that he accomplished it between visitations post-divorce.

These astounded women remark on what fantastic fathers and co-parents these former spouses are. The doctor reworked his schedule and cleared his weekends for his kids. He is very involved doing science experiments and other enjoyable educational activities. Cedric still has fun with his buddies, but spends quality time with his youngsters. He enjoys them and is completely focused on them during visitation. Eddie no longer leaves the parenting only to "Mum" but takes responsibility for them, goes over homework and attends parent/teacher conferences. Other women have echoed this same message about good co-parenting with their exes.

Do not be surprised if envy and anger play a part in co-parenting. The divorce may not have been your idea and now you have to share your children with other people. You miss them and may resent their time spent away from you. Acknowledge these natural emotions first before moving through them to get to a better state.

Emily got divorced several decades ago from a husband who left her for another woman. Her sons live across the country with the grandkids, so time is precious when they return home for visits. Soon these family members are going to the Caribbean to be with their father and stepmother in their condo. Not only does Emily feel left out, but is envious of their stepmother having many lazy days with them. Emily vented this resentment to friends and came up with a plan. She will be the "granny nanny" at one son's house while the parents get caught up with missed work after they return. Her son and daughter-in-law will be at their offices late, which gives Emily plenty of time to entertain her grandchildren. She is dealing with these emotions in a constructive way.

Co-parenting is a skill which is learned by trial and error. Give both of you some slack to make missteps, especially in the beginning. I have talked to and read about former couples who really like their exes' new partners, and getting together for birthday parties and other events is enjoyable. A woman said that one of her closest friends is her ex-husband's new wife. He married someone just like her, so they get along great.

Parental Alienation

Parental alienation syndrome is when a parent deliberately tries to turn a child against the other one. An indicator of this is when the child has had good relationships with both parents before the divorce, and has great animosity towards one now. A parent is verbally attacking the absent one and the children form an alliance with the attacker.

A component of parental alienation is that a parent may block or limit access to the other one, sometimes feeling justified because child support may be sporadic. This action is hindering the child's bond with the absent parent, who is being portrayed as inferior. Also a parent falsely accuses the other one of abuse or at least negligence. I have heard parents in the schools say how sick their children are after returning from the co-parent's house. Wanting school staff to take parental sides is totally inappropriate and affects children's education. If abuse is a concern, then discuss this with one's solicitor or doctor in a non-emergency situation. Document any instances of parental alienation, such as nasty texts or e-mails. Save any voice mails that belittle your parenting. Talk to your lawyer, about your concerns regarding this issue, since a court hearing may be necessary in this situation.

Polarization is when children are strongly attached to one parent and have a poor relationship with the other one. This is not a sudden occurrence, as in parental alienation. Polarization is a warning sign to investigate this circumstance more closely to see if it resulted from abuse. It also can be a safety issue where a child is afraid of extreme anger. A parent could be having a problem with impairment and requires medical attention. Determine the cause of polarization in case intervention is needed. Polarization is not because of a parent interfering with the relationship between the child and other parent. A divorce professional can differentiate between alienation and polarization.

14

Divorce and Co-Parenting with People Having Personality Disorders

Narcissist

Narcissists have an inflated self-image and expect the rest of the world to share this perceived importance. They are the star on the stage of life and others are bit players. They can be charming and charismatic, until they get what they want. When their mask slips, they become as cold as a robot. They crave continual admiration and exaggerate their accomplishments to cover up for their low self-esteem. Their sense of entitlement pushes them to rub elbows with their social superiors.

They tear down people to build themselves up, and may have stomped all over their spouse's self-esteem. They do not respect boundaries, and woe to anyone who tries to share their limelight. The key to divorcing these people is to give them the illusion that they are important and in control of the process.

The divorce process is supposed to revolve around their needs, wants, and schedule. In one divorce, both attorneys had to tip-toe around the narcissistic spouse to keep him in the collaborative process. The attorney's strategy was to encourage the wife to give in to small issues quickly, to prevent difficulties with larger ones down the road. She also massaged the narcissist's ego by asking about a recent trip or event. This fed the narcissist's need for "admiration" and made the sessions go smoother. Seeing a life coach may be helpful to a vulnerable spouse in order to feel more empowered during divorce.

Several esteemed psychologists said that children can be used as pawns, and recommend supervised visitation with the parent who is a narcissist. I know of one boy who insisted upon supervised visitation in this situation. It was granted, but he still could not tolerate being treated as an object by someone incapable of having a human connection. This went to court post-divorce and visitation was eventually terminated. A narcissistic parent lies, blames, and does put-downs. This can be confusing to a child, especially if the other parent is blamed as the sole cause of the divorce. A child in visitation may do well seeing a therapist.

A narcissist can use a child to obtain something, such as retaliation. He/she will fight for sole custody as a way to get a bigger financial settlement. He may play the good daddy role and parade the children around in front of clients and co-workers. This is an example of narcissistic extension, where the parent controls a child to bring himself praise and recognition. A parent may live through the child's achievements and view kids as a smaller version of themselves. Some beauty queens have narcissistic mothers who bask in the fame of these youngsters.

One father had obtained a black belt in Tai Kwon Do when in college, and made himself very visible when his son was following in his footsteps. When his son wanted to chase his dream of playing baseball, the narcissistic father went ballistic. His son was forced to stay in martial arts, and the father continued getting praise for his assistance, and for being such a great parent. Another narcissistic father lived through his son and kept him in Boy Scouts to earn his Eagle Scout Award, as he had done many decades ago. This father gained praise from other parents for his knowledge on many subjects for the badges. Finally the therapist mandated that this boy leave scouts, since it was only about the father and was causing so much distress.

Problem: How to have visitation be more successful with a narcissistic parent

Solution: Be extra careful not to make disparaging remarks about the other parent. Your child may hear plenty of them on visitation. Your kids may want extra time to themselves after transition between homes.

- When contact is shorter in duration without overnights, it can be better for all parties involved. If the activities are mutually interesting such as practicing a sport, then time spent together is more enjoyable. Attending a concert or film requires less interaction and is entertaining.
- One son requested going to his father's buddy's house during visitation. Then the teenager could talk to others and his father did not put down his mother in front of this audience. Another strategy is to set up visitation at a relative's house, where the child feels safe. When one narcissistic parent also had an impairment issue, visitation was formally set up at his mother's house overnight. The daughter saw her father there once a week in a safe setting.
- It is imperative that children having unsupervised contact with a narcissistic parent have someone monitoring this situation, whether it is a therapist, coach or godparent. Children can pick up on the parental behaviours that they witness and repeat this cycle in their own lives. The son who was not allowed to play baseball, had been controlled

by his parent. He picked two roommates in a row who manipulated and controlled his money, free-time activities and so forth. Finally he heeded his family and friends' advice and broke this pattern with short-term therapy.

Passive-aggressive

Another challenge in divorce and co-parenting, is dealing with a passive-aggressive spouse. They usually avoid direct confrontation, so it is difficult to know if they are angry. They appear calm on the surface while intense emotions are lurking underneath. Hostility is expressed indirectly through sneaky actions. This translates into longer and more expensive divorce proceedings. They may sabotage the divorce by seemingly going along with the process, but later refusing to sign papers. They often agree to something and then do not follow through with it. They may "forget" to bring needed documents to divorce sessions. They say that they forgot about it as a way to deflect another person's anger. They specialize in the silent treatment. During divorce, they may barely mumble an answer.

While co-parenting, a passive-aggressive person may return kids late from visitation. They may forget to take the youngsters to special events. Your alimony check is chronically late. They do not follow through with agreed upon tasks, and punish you for perceived infractions. He/she blames others, so everything is your fault, and on the job, co-workers are blamed for messing up their life. You are the perceived villain who caused the divorce and ruined their life, so you will be punished indirectly.

Problem: The ex is chronically late with visitation times

Solution: Get as much written in the divorce decree itself to avoid complications post-divorce. It is good to have direct deposits for child support set up with these types of parents. Alert your attorney about late payments to see if his wage can be garnished in the specified amount. Have a detailed Parenting Plan.

- Instead of having them pick up the kids at your place, with all of you peeking out the window, have it somewhere else. Some cities globally, such as London, have "Contact Centres" where kids can be dropped off and picked up. There are trained volunteers that can monitor visitation in a homey atmosphere.
- Another option is to have visitation at the paternal grandparents' house. This arrangement is working out well for one family, so when the passive-aggressive parent is late or forgetful it does not cause stress for the mother or kids. The mother drops off the youngsters and fetches them later. They have a blast with their grandparents and visiting cousins.
- See if a mediator can amend visitation. Find out legally the length of time required to wait for a pick up, so you are not in contempt of court if you and the kids go do an activity. Being late can be a way of retaliation regarding the divorce. Remove yourself from their game playing tactics.

Sociopath

The term sociopath is also referred to as antisocial personality disorder. These people can be charming while they are pursuing their goals. One may have been swept off her feet by this charisma while dating. These people are cold and ruthless behind their mask and have no remorse or compassion for others. Their sense of entitlement causes them to manipulate vulnerable people, including their own children, to get whatever they desire. Sociopaths can be reckless and impulsive and are highly represented in the prison populations. These individuals are often highly intelligent, and select careers which give them power over others, such as being a politician, surgeon, trial attorney, clergy or police.

They blame others and do not see the need to change, so are not prone to seeking therapy. They can erupt with rage, which is frightening for their children. These labile moods and disparaging remarks are a form of emotional abuse. They have no scruples so will try to enlist their kids into doing illegal or immoral acts with them. One sociopath father showed his young sons internet pornography acting as if this was a normal father/son activity. He threatened them not to tell their mother, or her divorcing him would be on their heads. When the younger son accidently let slip what their father had recently shown them, she called her husband. He denied it and the mother stated that an investigation would be started. The father left her a day later. This woman's divorce attorney asked why the father "couldn't have picked another hobby, like bowling with the kids."

These people do not respect life and may have a history torturing or killing animals. Get your pets out of the house when leaving. One woman's young pet died under mysterious circumstances a few months before they got a divorce. Antisocial personality disorder can have a genetic link, according to new research on this subject, so may be present in some families.

In divorce, a sociopath turns the charm on full blast to convince the judge to give them more assets or shared time.

One woman was divorcing a sociopath who did the blushing country boy act. The judge stated in court, that he did not know which spouse to believe since their stories were quite opposite. The wife had to fight to get her pre-marriage bank account back into her possession.

Sociopaths are the ones in the news who wipe out their family during an acrimonious divorce. They are also the stalkers who are the bane of celebrities.

Be cognizant of your safety and never let the sociopath into your home for any reason. If you stayed in the marital house, make sure that the locks, garage and alarm codes have been changed. If you feel in danger, act immediately. Call 911 (US), 999 (UK), your attorney, the police, or domestic abuse shelter, and possibly get a restraining order. You may need to modify visitation to have it supervised. You and your children's safety is paramount. Do not allow pick up or drop off at your house, but rather select a neutral location. I did not allow my sons to mention anything about me or our shared lives during their visitation with their father. I keep my life private from him.

Problem: Trying to work with a co-parent who has antisocial personality disorder

Solution: Have frequent and open communication with your children about what is happening in their lives. Have someone else available to confide in also, if they are not in therapy. Discuss what behaviour and ethics are acceptable and what is not.

• Volunteer with your kids, so they learn to express compassion to animals and develop empathy for those less fortunate in the community. Have them select a global charity for a family donation. This helps to offset the uncaring messages from the other parent. Giving back to others is a form of connection, which is a trait that people with personality disorders lack.

• The other parent may spew vile remarks about other ethnic groups or people not like him/her. A way to offset this is to take kids travelling to meet folks of other cultures. Children learn that humans globally have similar challenges and share many similar traits. Going to international festivals introduces kids to many customs and beliefs closer to home which is easier on the budget.

• Avoid talking with an antisocial personality disorder co-parent directly and keep communication to impersonal e-mails. Better to use an intermediary, such as a mediator, to handle all communication between both of you. Document interactions with this antisocial co-parent and what the children reveal, in case it is needed later in court. Give extra hugs and praise, because they may not be getting this from their other parent. Bestow unconditional love on your kids.

• Acting out a little in a divorce situation is normal, but being a juvenile delinquent is not. If you are told that your child is being extremely cruel and not respecting other kids, this is a red flag. "Conduct disorder" in children can be a precursor to antisocial personality disorder and early intervention by an experienced psychiatrist or psychologist may prevent it from becoming full blown. In therapy, parameters for behaviour are made with specific consequences. The child may gain insight during therapy, to prevent becoming a sociopath, if diagnosed with conduct disorder.

Make sure you and the kids have lightness and levity in your lives. Some routines are good such as going to grandma's for her spaghetti night. Fun and physical activity reduces stress when dealing with this difficult co-parent.

15

Dealing with Anger

Recognize that anger is a natural reaction to unreasonable demands in the divorce situation and take time to process this emotion. You may have moved, got a new job, and are seeing your children part-time. Anger is a stage in the grief cycle and one moves through it sooner or later. Here are some tips on resolving it sooner.

The Dalai Lama stated, "If we live our lives by anger and hatred, even our physical health deteriorates." It is how one deals with anger that impacts one's health. A study at Ohio State University demonstrated the effects of anger on wound healing and the immune system. Forty-two couples married over ten years were studied on two separate occasions where blisters were induced by suction cups. The first time the discussion was general and the second time it was regarding stressful topics on which the couple disagreed. Blisters were monitored and blood was drawn to determine the cytokine level. Cytokine helps wounds to heal and is a marker for the immune system. The more hostile couples' blisters took an extra day, or 1 ½ times longer to heal. You want cytokine to be at the wound level for healing. When it is elevated in the blood (as with hostile people), then this can lead to inflammation which worsens arthritis and other diseases.

Anger activates stress hormones, which in turn raise the blood pressure and heart rate. Cleveland Clinic's Psychologies Testing Center found that it "causes wear and tear on the heart and cardiovascular system." Is being angry at your ex worth a possible stroke or heart attack?

Problem: How to let go of anger

Solutions: Think of anger as pressurized steam which needs to be released periodically, rather than leading to an explosion. Anger can be a barrier that keeps people away – just when one needs them the most.

• Write a scathing letter to your spouse listing the many transgressions and how he or she was cruel. Get everything out onto paper. State your feelings and anything else that comes to mind. Notice how a burden has been lifted and you feel better when this task is completed. However do not send it. Tear the letter into little bits, burn it, or pick another way to destroy it. The point is getting your fury out in writing, as a means to move on. This exercise works well for toxic people in your life, from your obnoxious boss to your former sister-in-law. My son was angry about a relative that was not supportive of us after my divorce, and chose to be in my former spouse's camp. That is her right to do so. My son wrote a blistering letter to her regarding his hurt feelings, and at the last minute decided not to mail it. A few days later, he remarked how much better he felt and that it was fine to part ways with this family member.

• My anger lessened when I took responsibility for my part in the demise of my marriage. Even if your spouse is Satan's spawn, both parties contributed to the divorce. Realize that you are not perfect and neither is your ex. After reaching this realization, my migraines dramatically decreased in frequency. When anger explodes, that leads to longer litigation and higher legal fees for both parties.

Having a strong emotion towards your ex is a form of attachment that is not therapeutic. Why stay attached?

• Physical activity lowers adrenaline (fight or flight response) leaving one feeling calmer. Taking a walk can lesson these angry feelings. Do yoga, or any movements to release this steam. So many people have shared about how taking an exercise class, or starting a new fitness routine, has changed their lives for the better. Instead of plotting revenge, they are plotting new jogging routes and activities.

• Abe had a lot of anger during a crumbling marriage and had one session of hypnotherapy. In this session, he learned to visualize his anger turning into a bouquet of flowers. He gave a form to the emotion of anger and transformed the original shape of it into the bouquet. Abe discovered how to identify the tension which manifests into fury, in order to stop anger in its tracks.

• A solution to releasing anger is by hitting something. One fellow routinely went to a batting cage during the tumultuous time before his divorce. After a nurse's break up, she imagined the dart board to be a picture of her ex's face. She gained prowess in this sport and won dart tournaments. This skill transferred into giving painless injections on the job and increased patient satisfaction.

• A TV show highlighted unusual entrepreneur enterprises. A woman smashed crockery on her driveway during her divorce. She realized how that released her pent-up anger. She opened a place in San Diego where people bought cheap china to smash during their break-ups or emotionally-charged times. A person would go into a specially designed room wearing protective gear to throw the glassware and china. Smiling customers were interviewed afterwards and stated that they felt so much better. Although this place has since closed, other ones opened globally, such as in Tokyo.

• Anne found cleaning the house was therapeutic for releasing anger during her acrimonious divorce. She scrubbed and tackled major jobs with gusto. Gemma got out her anger and frustrations by cleaning her flat during divorce, and appreciated a gleaming residence as a bonus. Anger can produce a jittery feeling which is dispelled by vigorous activities.

Anger wastes time and energy that could be used in a more beneficial way. Your own anger can ignite your spouse's anger in divorce, which hampers the proceedings. No matter how much I felt like exploding, my demeanour remained calm so it was not apparent to my husband that he was pushing my buttons during the collaborative sessions. Anger keeps one anchored in the past. A ship cannot move on to a new destination while still moored in port. Let go and sail on.

Anger in Children

Even if children are relieved that the divorce is happening (as I was at age four), their lives will still be in an upheaval. Model the behaviour that you want your kids to emulate. If you are screaming or exploding like a volcano – then that may exacerbate their own angry reactions. Release your anger away from the youngsters and strive to be calm in their presence.

When kids are acting out, use "I" statements. "I do not feel appreciated when you yell at me." We get so absorbed in our own struggle that we can be less focused on the children. Sometimes their naughty behaviour is a call to get our attention. I found that being honest with my sons went a long way in maintaining a calmer atmosphere. I informed them when I was feeling extra stressed and needed a time out to read.

Keep in mind a child's age when dealing with their anger. Younger kids may want to express their frustration through drawing. Older ones may appreciate a break from both parents and would enjoy some fun with a godparent.

Look for signs that kids may not be adapting in a healthy way to the divorce. If their grades take a nose dive, or they drop out of all activities, then talk to their teacher for some feedback. If they change friends and are hanging out with juvenile delinquents, then do some investigating. Your kids may be dabbling in drugs or alcohol. Keep tabs on the kids without micromanaging. One recently divorced mother had to call the police when her teenager became violent.

Keeping lines of communication open and possibly having the children meet with a children's divorce coach can help them deal with their anger. A neutral third party can assist with formulating coping strategies and helping them express strong emotions in a healthier manner.

Reprinted with permission from The Divorce Magazine UK
By Wendi Schuller

Divorce Through Children's Eyes

Parents may feel that they are sailing through divorce, yet children can view it quite differently. As a part-time school nurse, I have listened to many children who end up in my nurse's office with stress induced health issues. Here is what kids wish their parents knew:

- **We are not property that has to be divided equally**. One youngster developed an eye twitch after his parents' divorce. They tried to be fair splitting assets and this carried over to shared care 50/50. The boy did not like the frequent switches to each parent's home. I spoke to the mother about this boy's concern. The parents were able to negotiate that he would spend 75% at his mum's and 25% with dad. His dad would be able to pick Aiden up at his mum's for an activity and return him there afterwards. The twitch went away with this new arrangement and Aiden enjoyed time with each parent.

- **Do not march into battle over us**. It may be appropriate in a Victorian novel to fight over a loved one, but not in this era. I had one student who spent all morning in my nurse's office while his parents went to war in court over custody that day. His teacher sent this lad to me, since he was incapable of learning in the classroom. Reassure the child that his custody wishes will be taken into consideration. Keep kids out of the divorce drama and do not share details with them.

- **We want to know that there will be some continuity in our lives**. Let the kids know that while divorce details are still being decided, the main points in their lives will remain the same. The children will attend their current schools and maintain contact with friends. They will still go to sports practices, dance classes, scouting, or whatever activities they participate in now.

- **We want some say in our lives**. Loss of control equals ending up in my nurse's office with headaches or stomach aches. While kids do not set boundaries or make the rules – they certainly can have some input. Let them help with family decisions, such as do we want a summer holiday, or spread treats out during the year and have a staycation? Ask what their priorities are and work on a strategy together on how to reach them.

- **Listen to us when we try and get your attention**. Do not let a small problem turn into a big one because you are barely able to keep your head above water. I have seen a few kids develop eating disorders after parents' divorces. Check in with your children at least weekly to let them air their concerns. Some do this at family meetings to discuss issues and go over the weekly schedule and upcoming events. Kids who feel lost in the shuffle may turn to the comfort of drugs and alcohol. When busy, doing parallel activities side by side with the kids still counts as spending time with them.

- **Please do not talk to me about the other parent or your frustrations with them**. Kids know our strengths and weaknesses and do not require having them pointed out by the other parent. I just tell my son that both of his parents have made mistakes and he can see what worked and use that when he becomes a parent.

- **Do not make excuses about the absent parent which gets our hopes up and confuses us about reality**. If a parent does not pick up the child for visitation or carries through on a promise, do not defend them. That can prolong agony or give false expectations when one parent wants to step out of the picture. You do not know what is going on in the absent parent's heart or mind, so do not give reassurances. Instead focus on the child. Acknowledge the child's feelings, saying that you can see she is disappointed/frustrated. Perhaps introduce a diversion, such as suggesting she call a friend now for a pizza sleepover.

If you feel that your children are not adjusting to the divorce situation, then consider taking them to meet with a divorce coach or therapist.

16

Men's Guide and Resources for Divorce

Some men have opted not to contribute to their retirement plans during their divorces, since their wives could be receiving half of them. If you do this, remember to start up the contributions after your divorce is finalized. Take your wife off as co-signer on your credit card. If you have a joint credit card, call the company and have them remove your name. Open a credit card in your name only. If your name is attached to department store and local credit cards, get your name off those as well.

Go to your financial institution and withdraw up to half of the funds and have your name removed from those bank accounts. Save the receipts for divorce proceedings. Some men have chosen to deposit those funds in their name only at a different bank. If you have a joint checking account, have your name removed from it. Check on any automatic withdrawals from your pay checks to a joint bank account for a paying a bill and stop these transactions. Your name may be removed from that joint account, but the payments still going via routing and bank account numbers to it.

Consider hiring your own personal financial advisor to look over any potential divorce agreements particularly if you are the high earner. Some investments seem similar on the surface, but the tax consequences may be different. Child support is not tax deductible to the payer as alimony is. See if you can pay tuition directly to schools as part of the child support; it may be a tax advantage to you. Do not quibble over the small stuff. Save your battles for the big ones. If you only would get a $50.00 tax advantage to claim your kids as deductibles, let your wife do this. You will seem magnanimous and may gain a better asset in exchange for this kindness.

Remember to change your will and remove your ex-wife as beneficiary from insurance policies, pension plans, and investments. When you remarry, redo your will and add your new wife's to your investments. Consider getting a pre-nuptial agreement made to protect your children's interests in your assets. Some parents have a trust set up with their offspring before marrying again. Consult with a financial planner to make the best decisions in your circumstance.

Sometimes people get divorced and rediscover each other decades later. They get remarried and live happily ever after as if in a fairy tale. In other instances whatever tore them apart the first time does so again. If you are tempted to reunite with your former spouse, get some pre-marital counselling first. This true story gives another twist to why exes occasionally get back together.

A couple without children had a Clean Break divorce in London and went their separate ways. Sven was originally from Sweden and Katia from Russia. This divorce involved millions of pounds, yet was fairly easy going. Post-divorce, Sven made quite a lot more money in successful business dealings. A bit later Sven started bumping into Katia who said that she had made a mistake and still loved him. Sven wooed Katia with expensive baubles and they got remarried. His friends and family tried to warn Sven that this looked a trap, but he chose not to heed their advice. Unbeknownst to Sven, Katia had gotten wind of his increased earnings and it was greed, not love that attracted her to Sven again. Eventually Katia divorced Sven and she got another big piece of the pie.

Make sure that you give your parents and other relatives time to see the children. If you have an urgent commitment during shared care, this would be a good opportunity to leave the kids with relatives. Some paternal grandparents have expressed frustration in the amount of time that they see their grandchildren post-divorce. Make sure your parents have regular contact with your kids since this is such a mutually beneficial relationship. Alert them to school events, sporting tournaments, and other activities in your children's lives.

Men can be stoic and may perceive asking for help or advice as a weakness. Meet mates at the pub and ask for their divorce stories after a pint. They may be able to steer you in the right direction for a lawyer, financial advisor, etc.

There are MeetUp.com groups for straight males who want companionship for activities. Being in one of these all-male groups gives camaraderie without any pressure to share personal problems. Some divorced fellows have joined sporting, hiking, and other outdoor groups for fun. *Talking Sticks* in Surrey, UK is an example of this. It can feel isolating being in a divorce, particularly if close friends are members of your wife's family or husbands of her close friends. Joining some male or mixed groups can widen your social network.

Some fellows pour themselves into work to focus their mind on other pursuits besides divorce. Look into expanding your professional network as well. If you have flexibility in your job, consider putting in more hours in when your children are with their mother. This can lighten up your schedule when you have them so you have more time for interaction and activities. See if work related travel can be planned far in advance so as not to coincide with your shared care time with your kids.

Be respectful and polite in divorce sessions and in co-parenting. There really is something to the cliché that one gets more flies with honey than vinegar. This honey could be more desirable assets or shared time. Emotions and attitudes are contagious so if you are adversarial or angry do not be surprised if your wife is too, during divorce proceedings.

See how you can shave a bit off your expenses. Have buddies over for beer and munchies to watch games at home rather than at expensive sports bars. Buy cheaper cuts of meat and marinade them for tenderness. See how you can slash your food bills. Buy great liquor and ale at cheaper places, such as at Trader Joe's. Some rave about their Scottish Whisky which is at a fraction of other's prices. Look at package plans for cheaper divorces, particularly in the UK. You can budget better without big surprises with these all-inclusive deals.

Read the chapter on travel with kids. There are special dad trips and single-parent tours. Your kids have fun with the other kids and you have a break with some adult time. Your kids may enjoy some low-cost travel adventures, such as camping out in a cool place. Consider introducing them to more outdoor pursuits, such as easy hikes in scenic areas.

Dads bring a sense of adventure and playfulness to their children's lives. Continue this in the post-divorce period. Even in the work place, it has been men that have made jobs more enjoyable with humour and fun. Guys have the gift of bringing levity to a difficult situation and diffusing any tension. As I nurse I see mums asking crying kids if they need to go to the hospital. The dads do first aid, and comment "You'll live" and the crying ceases quickly. When kids are in foul moods it is the dads who excel in distraction to get them out of that funk. Kids are under stress with divorce and need lightness in their lives.

In bringing fun to kids' lives do not fall into the trap of the "Disneyland Dad" who is only about good times and does not enforce boundaries or rules. It is more difficult to be in the parental role, rather than the good buddy one. Children's lives are turned upside down with divorce and consistency with rules helps. Out-of-control children are not happy and require having a parent to be in charge. Find your balance between fun and games and exerting your parental authority.

Many women in high places have said that they owed their success to their fathers. These men gently pushed them to achieve their goals when it did not seem possible at the time. Their fathers urged them to take risks and picked them up when they fell. Sometimes we mothers see obstacles and danger, and fathers see the big picture. Your children will benefit from these unique qualities.

You may have a difficult former wife who does not collaborate well as a co-parent. Children can see their parents' strengths and foibles. Men I interviewed said that they stuck it out when their exes made contact difficult or bad mouthed them to the kids. One father said that he barely had enough to eat due to paying child support. The joy is that his kids eventually realized that and have such a close relationship with him. He said the sacrifices were worth it in the end, with the strong bonds he forged throughout kids' childhood.

It is upsetting to share kids and not be a day-to-day father. Be involved in their lives between visitations. Check when their practices and games are happening so that you can attend. Consider Skyping or having designated times to call them when they are with their mother. Let the children know that you are available in between their shared care times with you. Email and text to keep in contact. Let your former wife know that you are happy to step in when she may have a work deadline, trip for business, or other commitments.

It may be hard to see her at events, especially with a new partner, but be polite, if not pleasant, to extend time spent with your kids. If she feels that you two can get along, then there may be more invitations given for mutual events, such as birthdays. What has helped some divorced people is to think of their former spouse as if they were a quirky relative. You no longer see your former wife on a day to day basis, so visualize her as a crotchety aunt whom you put up with on occasion for the sake of the kids. Others mentally view their ex as an exaggerated cartoon character or a caricature, which enables them to seem silly rather than annoying.

Some fathers have been coaches, scout leaders, Big Brothers and other mentors to youth between visitations. This has helped fill the void that is left in their lives without daily face-to-face contact with the kids. Others have volunteered at their children's schools for events and projects. Being active helps stave off those depressing thoughts of not seeing the kids 24/7.

There are many resources specifically for men. Here is a partial list:

Men's Divorce @mensdivorcenews
We believe everyone deserves equal treatment in family law, so we strive to educate men on how to protect themselves before, during and after divorce.

The Good Men Project @GoodMenProject
We're starting a conversation about what it means to be a good man. Want to join us? info@GoodMenProject.com

Cordell & Cordell @CordellLaw

Cordell & Cordell is a family law firm dedicated to helping men in divorce, custody cases, and protecting fathers' rights with offices in 30 states. Have helpful articles for men globally.

Dads Divorce @dadsdivorce
Dads Divorce is run by the divorce attorneys at Cordell & Cordell. Cordell and Cordell and Dads Divorce support fathers in family law, child custody and divorce

Fathers 4 Justice @Fathers4Justice
Bringing INTERNATIONAL awareness to archaic ANTI-Family draconian judicial systems which abuse children for their own financial gain. JUSTICE IS COMING!!!

Fathers4Justice @F4JOfficial United Kingdom
The Official #Fathers4Justice Campaign Organisation founded by Matt O'Connor in 2001. Fixing the Fatherless Society / Campaigning for #SharedParenting

FathersSupportGroup @FathersSupportG
FatherSupportGroup Based in South London Fighting for equal rights in the court room Help and emotional support 07717597310

Father Mag.com @fathermag
Fathering Magazine at http://FatherMag.com - The online father magazine for dads, since 1996.

Divorce Support for Men Meetup Groups - Meetup
divorce-support-for-men.meetup.com

Find Meetups about **Divorce Support** for **Men** and meet people in your local community who share your interests.

Men and Divorce - DivorceInfo

www.**divorce**info.com/**men**and**divorce**.htm

Men going through **divorce** have made perhaps more aggressive use of the Internet than any other **group** dealing with the crud of **divorce**. Web sites abound from **men** ...

Men's Advocacy-Counseling: How We Can Help You

www.nationalcenterfor**men**.org/page2.shtml

The National Center For **Men**, incorporated in 1987, is dedicated to the **advocacy** of **men's** equal rights. We educate the public about how **men** have been hurt by sex ...

Men's and Father's Rights - Divorce Source: divorce ...

www.divorcesource.com › Categories

The **Men's Rights** Manual for **Divorce** What you are experiencing or contemplating is probably going to be the most difficult time of your life. Separation and **divorce** ...

Facilitated groups for men - Menstuff

www.**men**stuff.org/resources/resourcefiles/**groups**-facilitated.html

Menstuff® has gathered the following facilitated **men's groups**. See also "**Men's** Council's" and **Groups** - Peer Facilitated. Not all states have reported a **men's groups**.

Men's Divorce - Divorce Forum and Child Custody Forum...

forum.**mensdivorce**.com

Divorce Forum and Child Custody **Forum**. Support and help for **men** and fathers before, during, and after **divorce**

Abused Men in Scotland (AMIS) is a national organisation dedicated to supporting men who are experiencing, or who have experienced, domestic abuse. http://www.abusedmeninscotland.org/index.html

17

Divorce in the UK

By Austin Chessell

Collaborative – How is collaborative divorce different in the UK? If at all.

Collaborative divorce in the UK works in a similar way to America.

Each client would select his or her own collaborative lawyer.

Each client and the lawyers would sign an agreement not to go to court.

There are no letters sent.

All of the points each client would like to discuss are carried out in face to face round the table meetings.

If an agreement were reached in collaborative law then the lawyers would prepare a financial consent order. This is then filed at the court to be approved by the Judge.

In the event that there is an impasse and collaborative law stops then each client would need to instruct a new lawyer to act for him or her.

The new lawyer could assist the clients in preparing a court application if it is decided court proceedings need to commence.

In terms of costs mediation tends to be more cost effective than Collaborative law but it depends what you want from the process when you are separating. The mediator cannot provide legal advice while the lawyer in collaborative law can. Also the collaborative law process provides a lot more privacy than court and you control the speed of the sessions. At court there may be a long waiting time for the matter to be listed and there could be several court hearings. It should also not be underestimated the stress attending court can create. Mediation and collaborative law tend to be more interest based to ensure that each party is considered while if you go to court it can get very positional in what each client is seeking. I am also finding in this economic climate that a lot of separating couples

are able to sit down and talk around the table themselves what they want as an agreement and then they just instruct a solicitor to document what has been agreed between them.

Litigation – Isn't there a waiting period before a divorce – or a time period before a divorce can be granted in the UK? Litigation seems to be the most different – more fault vs no fault divorce as in USA. Any more differences?

In the UK you have to be married for one year before divorce proceedings can commence.

You may also want to consider if the marriage can be annulled but only certain situations apply to this.

If the divorce is uncontested the divorce process is normally three – four months. The Petitioner usually has three sets of forms to complete for the court and the Respondent has one form to fill in.

The middle point of the divorce (Decree Nisi) once this is granted by the court you need to wait 6 weeks and a day before the divorce is finalized. Also a lot of separating couples wait until the financial agreement is reached and sealed by the court before applying to complete the divorce (Decree Absolute).

If you wait over a year after Decree Nisi is granted before applying for the Decree Absolute you would need to provide the court with a short statement explaining why there was a delay in completing the final divorce application.

Depending on the circumstance of the divorce you may apply for a fault or non-fault based divorce. Fault based may be unreasonable behaviour or adultery. I aim to ask clients where possible to get the divorce petition approved by their former partner before the divorce petition is sent to court. I find that the former partner is more likely to be cooperative with the divorce if they are consulted and also it reduces the likelihood of the divorce petition needing to be amended. If the court papers are needing to be amended there will be a court fee and also extra legal costs if you have instructed a solicitor.

I try to also agree with the former partner how the divorce costs will be shared between them. If this cannot be agreed then there is the chance for both the Petitioner and Respondent to attend court to explain what costs they feel they should pay towards the divorce before the Judge makes a decision.

In most uncontested divorces where there are no disagreements normally the spouses do not need to attend court.

It is not always possible to apply for a non-fault based divorce in the UK. Where it is possible it can then help to make negotiations easier for the children and financial aspects of the case so bear in mind if you want to go for the fault based divorce it may make it harder to resolve other aspects of the divorce if the other spouse is made angry by what is said in the divorce petition.

When I mediate with clients they can talk through who will start the divorce and what the details will be in the petition so that there will be no surprises. Also the timing of when the divorce papers are served can be discussed. I have mediated with couples who have been very upset to receiving divorce papers on special dates or holidays and if this is talked through with the former partner in advance this can avoid upsetting the former partner.

Mediation

Mediation Information Assessment Meetings

Legal aid has stopped for family law matters in the UK apart from certain exceptions e.g. domestic violence or child abduction.

Legal aid still remains for family mediation if you are eligible.

On the 22nd April 2014, there was a change in the law that it is now necessary for Applicants to attend a Mediation Information Assessment Meeting (MIAM) if they intend to make a financial or children application at court. There will only be exceptional circumstances when a court application will be allowed to be issued without the assessment of suitability for mediation being carried out first.

As a family mediator I have found that there has been a good uptake of cases converting into family mediation sessions once they know how the process works and what the benefits of mediation are over going to court.

Mediation International Relocation Case example

Not every international relocation case has to go to court.

I recently worked with a couple who lived in Central London.

They were married for 20 years and had two children aged 12 and 16.

The wife wanted to join her new partner in Canada and leave London. It was agreed that the 12 year old would go and live with the mother in Canada.

It was also agreed that the 16 year old would live with the father in London.

They agreed to a 50/50 split of the assets.

There was a flexible plan agreed as to how childcare would work during the holidays.

I had two mediation sessions to reach the childcare and financial proposals.

The clients sought legal and financial advice in between the sessions before a final proposal was documented. Advice was also sought from abroad to see if the final decision could be mirrored into a Canadian legal document too.

The clients wanted to avoid going to court and minimise the costs associated with separation. They also wanted to divorce in a holistic way that would not damage the family. Mediation helped to achieve their aims.

Shared Care

Sometimes shared care of the children can work on a 50/50 basis. However the parents need to consider what will work best for the child as shared care does not necessarily mean the child will spend 50% of the time with each parent.

You need to consider how old the child is and what is being proposed is it right for a child of this age.

Logistically what is being proposed for childcare you need to ask yourself will it work.

The childcare arrangement should not leave the child feeling worn out especially if the child has school the next day.

If the child is deemed old enough and the parents are in mediation, if the parents consent the mediator can have a session with the child to find out what their wishes and feelings are. The child can then let the mediator know what information they agree for the mediator to tell the parents. This may then help to shape how future childcare arrangements will work.

Post Divorce Considerations

When you receive the Decree Absolute from the court to confirm the divorce has been completed and the sealed financial consent order there may be other practicalities and emotional points that you still need to consider. The below list is not everything but tends to be common points clients should bear in mind.

1. If you have received a financial lump sum as part of the divorce settlement you may want to consider speaking to a financial advisor who can discuss with you how to invest the lump sum.

2. If you have an old will you may want to now get this updated or if you do not have a will consider having a will prepared.

3. Have you carried out all the steps requested of you in the financial consent order? If you have not the former partner may seek enforcement against you and possibly a costs order from court if you do not follow the dates set out in the court order so it is important to ensure the financial order has been complied with.

4. Have you informed the children's school and their networks that the divorce has recently been completed and at this point in time the children may need extra support and understanding. Sometimes I have a mediation session with the children if the parents think this would be useful and then feedback what the children agree or ask me to tell the parents.

5. Do you feel that now the legal matters have been dealt with that it could be a good time to speak to a counsellor or therapist to deal with the emotional issues to try and make the future as smooth as possible? Not every client feel that they need this but it is something to consider.

6. If you had any joint bank account(s) with your former partner have they now been closed?

7. If you find it difficult to talk to your former partner you may want to consult a divorce coach to explore ways on how to communicate effectively with them going forwards. Especially if you have children you are going to need to liaise with your former partner about how the childcare will work and evolve, you will also be attending events such graduations and the children's weddings together so even if you have now separated you should aim to put on a unified front when present with the children.

8. Have you detailed in the financial consent order how the more expensive items are to be divided so that when you come to moving out of the former matrimonial home there is not a reason for disagreements to break out over who should retain each item. An annex listing who retains each item can be attached to the consent order for the court. I have also had mediation sessions with couples to talk through who takes which item as this can be more cost effective than there being a lot of solicitor correspondence or a court application to resolve this matter.

9. If you are relocating abroad as part of the divorce does the order need to be written into an order abroad too by a foreign lawyer so that the terms of the divorce, children and financial settlement are mirrored in both jurisdictions?

10. If you are planning to remarry fairly soon after the divorce has been completed have you considered having a prenuptial agreement prepared? They are not legally binding in the UK but this is currently being reviewed. You may have been through a bitter and expensive divorce through the courts and would want to aim to avoid having a repeat of this happening again in the event that the new marriage was to break down. Or there may be a big wealth imbalance that you want to aim to protect in the event that the new relationship

International Law

Austin Chessell looks at some of the main principles of the law on International Relocation and discusses how parents can use them in family mediation as an alternative to going to court to help them shape their own agreement on whether relocation with children should take place

This article was first published in Solicitors Journal in November 2013 and is reproduced by kind permission.

With the growth in cheap flights and increasing employment prospects arising from globalisation it is becoming more common for separated parents to consider permanently relocating abroad and wanting to take their children with them. Consent needs to be given by the non-relocating parent for the relocation to take place which is rarely easy to obtain as it inevitably creates further tension between the parents and re-opens the pain experienced during the initial post separation childcare discussions. The non-relocating parent often fears losing all contact with the child if relocation happens. Where relocation is contested, it is worth considering what the main legal principles are which determine whether the relocation should take place and whether consent is best obtained through the courts or by mediation. In my experience, mediation is often more successful where parents have a good understanding of these legal principles and can then use them to shape their own relocation agreements.

The leading cases which parents need to be aware of are:
Payne v Payne [2001] EWCA Civ 166

This was an unsuccessful appeal by a father against an order allowing the mother (who significantly was the main carer) to remove the child to New Zealand. The guidance in this case is known as the 'Payne Test.'

The test means that the court must consider if the proposed relocation:

* derives from a genuine desire to start a new life abroad (i.e. not being selfishly motivated to cut one parent out of the child's life)

* has been well thought out and researched having regard to the practicalities of the situation.

If the application to relocate is deemed to be genuine and realistic, the court must then weigh up:

* if the opposing parent's reasons are based on a genuine concern for the future child's welfare, or if there is an ulterior motive.

* what effect the relocation would have on the relationship between the parent who is not relocating and the child. The court will also need to consider the extent to which this would be balanced by any new relationships that the child would form in the relocation country.

* What the impact would be on the parent who proposed the move if the application was refused.

While taking the guidance into account, the court's paramount concern will always be the child's welfare.

However, in Re K [2011] EWCA Civ 793 the Court of Appeal ruled that the only point of law from the Payne case was that the child's best interests must be the paramount consideration of the court. In this case, (unlike Payne) care was shared between the parents. The court decided that in shared care

cases the application should be decided on the facts of each case, the welfare of the child and the statutory considerations which are set out in s.1(3) of the Children Act 1989,often referred to as the 'Welfare Checklist'.

In Re K a father brought a successful appeal against an order which gave the mother permission to leave and take the children to Canada. The court confirmed that in the circumstances of this case the approach followed in Payne v Payne was not appropriate because care was shared between the parents which require a deeper analysis of the impact of the relocation on the child. As a result of this case a lot of parents may now find it harder to persuade the court that the relocation should take place where there is a shared care arrangement in place.

Payne is only applicable where the relocating parent is the main carer. The approach in Payne should not be followed where the parents share the caring of the children in more or less equal proportions. Consideration must be given to all of the facts.

Key findings from relocation case law are:
* The welfare of the child is the paramount consideration and all other criteria should feed into this.
* In deciding which solution will best meet the child's welfare, consideration should be given to the guidance set out in the Welfare Checklist where care is shared and to the Payne Test where there is a main carer for the child.

* Leave to remove applications must be made in a way which does not obstruct contact nor weaken the child's relationship with the non-relocating parent.

* The relocating parent must have planned the move having regard to the practicalities e.g. it is better if the move is at the end of the school year rather than in the middle of the school term, having good access to healthcare, immigration laws not being a major obstacle and the non-relocating parent still being able to still have good contact with the child.

* The court will have regard to the impact which a refusal of the application will have on the relocating parent where s/he is the primary carer, e.g. the primary carer feeling isolated and lonely if the move is not granted.

* It is important in every case to consider what the effect of the reduction in contact time with the parent who is not relocating will be on the child.

* If the child is an older child then its wishes, views and feelings will carry more weight in the relocation decision.

As a mediator my role is different to when I am acting as a solicitor in that in mediation I can only share the above legal information with mediation clients but cannot advise them. Parents can then use that information and seek legal advice from solicitors where appropriate to make joint decisions on the relocation through mediation.

In August 2013, Dr Rob George from Oxford University found in a report called Relocation Disputes in England and Wales: First Findings from the 2012 Study that one third of all requests for relocation are not permitted by the family courts. In the current economic climate parents are questioning why they should spend potentially tens of thousands of pounds on a relocation case involving several hearings when the case can be mediated in a quicker and more cost effective way (especially where a relocation allowance has not been provided by an employer) and, in light of Dr George's report, may stand a higher chance of success.

Every mediation case is unique based on the client's circumstances, but the following are issues that commonly arise in international relocation cases which parents (and mediators) need to consider:

* Childcare time - when should the contact take place and where?

* Who is booking and paying for the international travel?

* If the child is young how will they travel? Will relatives need to be involved to ensure travel can take place.

* Will contact between the child and the non-relocating parent take place during term time and in what form. .e.g. face to face, email, phone or Skype?

* Making decisions for future education, after school activities and medical treatments - it may be that the parent who is not relocating wants to visit the school abroad or neighbourhood before any schooling decisions are made.

* Being provided with copies of future medical records and school reports.

* If an order is prepared after mediation, will this need to be mirrored abroad? The clients will need to liaise with their legal advisors here and abroad to get this confirmed.

* If the order is not followed, should the relocating parent provide a legal costs allowance for the parent who is not relocating? There may not be funds for this but in some cases there may be.

* Will the parent not relocating have more contact prior to the move?

* Will the parent agree for the relocation to be for a defined time before returning?

* Will the children return in the future for their university education? If the children are old enough and the parents agree, the mediator can meet with the children to find out their wishes and feelings on this and then pass agreed information back to the parents before a decision is made.

* How will extended family members remain involved with the children?

* Will the relocation take place in a way that is not disruptive to the child?

I have worked on relocation cases through the courts as a solicitor and through mediation as a family mediator. In my experience parents communicate better in mediation than they do in litigation as the focus is on collective interests not fixed positions. If a parent is unhappy with a court decision, litigation will most likely continue with appeals being made, but, in mediation, parents tend to respect what was agreed and rarely look to amend a Memorandum of Understanding.

With Mediation Information Assessment Meetings (MIAMs)likely to become compulsory for all applicants if the Children and Families Bill 2012-2013 is enacted, it would not be surprising if more international relocation cases are resolved through mediation rather than through the court system.

Austin Chessell is a Collaborative Family Solicitor at Feltons Solicitors in Knightsbridge, London. He is also a Child and Family Mediator at FAMIA across inner and greater London. Email: achessell@feltonssolicitors.co.uk & austin.chessell@famia.co.uk

Austin Chessell - Collaborative Family Solicitor - Feltons Solicitors, Knightsbridge - London.

Austin Chessell is a consultant Family Solicitor and Family Mediator at Feltons Solicitors. He has been working in the field of Family Law since 2005.

Austin aims to find the right divorce option for the client and for the divorce to be done in a dignified way to ensure that the family is kept intact.

Austin acts for middle to high net worth clients and increasingly more of his cases have an international element. He deals with children, financial and divorce matters.

Austin trained as a Family Mediator in 2009 and formed FAMIA in 2010 with Massy Ellesmere. He is also trained to mediate with children where appropriate so that their wishes and feelings can be informed to the parents. Austin can also provide Mediation Information Assessment Meetings (MIAMs) to mediation clients and is authorised to provide FM1 forms.

He is committed to resolving matters out of court and trained as a Collaborative Lawyer in 2013 with Resolution. Austin is a member of the Collaborative Pod Essex Family Solutions and works closely with counsellors, therapists, mediators and independent financial advisors as part of the divorce process.

Austin provides a choice of all the divorce options:- Family Mediation, Collaborative Law and Court. If you have resolved a matter on your own (DIY discussions) Austin can provide advice on what you have decided.

If you want to have your matter decided by Arbitration Austin can suggest to you one of his known and trusted Arbitration colleagues.

Austin does litigate when necessary but most of his cases settle out of court or reach an agreement before a final hearing. Austin is very client focussed.

Austin is a regular writer for Solicitors Journal for fellow professionals.

He was a Trustee for the charity Families Need Fathers (FNF) from 2011 – 2014.

Austin provides Family Law and Family Mediation Information at legal clinics for FNF in London and at the RCJ advice bureau in Holborn.

Austin has formed a children contact centre in the past. He has been a volunteer for supported contact and was a sessional worker for supervised cases from 2005 – 2013. He is very empathetic to the issues surrounding a family separation for the children and the parents.

Austin has formed a thriving London Family Mediation Group in 2011 for Family Mediators which meets four times a year in Central London. New members are welcome.

He is a member of Resolution, The Family Mediators Association and the International Academy of Collaborative Professionals.

Email address: achessell@feltonssolicitors.co.uk

5

Scottish Law Contribution

By Anne Hall Dick

Although a separating Scottish couple face the same emotional journey as a separating couple anywhere, the legal landscape they have to navigate is very specific to Scotland.

The legal rules in Scotland for financial provision on divorce

Where married couples (and since 2014 that can include same sex marriage in Scotland) or civil partners (which in Scotland will only involve same sex partners) separate the most usual approach is to use some form of negotiation to tackle the things which have to be sorted out. Plans are captured in a formal registered document called a Separation Agreement or a Minute of Agreement. Only a Court can grant a divorce or dissolve a Civil Partnership. Although ending a marriage or Civil Partnership is always a significant step, if there is a formal Agreement in place the divorce itself is not legally complex once you have been separated for a year if you both want a divorce. The Court granting the divorce doesn't have to approve the financial arrangements.

If you are not able to agree the financial side, when you ask the Court for a divorce or to end a Civil partnership you ask the Court to decide the financial arrangements as well. The Court applies legal rules to do that. Those rules are not binding on couples who sort things out by agreement but they are usually used as a measure of fairness in negotiations. They are guidelines rather than a straitjacket in negotiations and only imposed if matters have to be sorted out in litigation.

The legal rules set out what should be included as matrimonial or partnership property. Anything acquired during the marriage by gift from a third party or from inheritance is not included. Neither are assets owned before the marriage or civil partnership (except a place to live or contents bought for use by you as a family home). However, if non matrimonial assets are sold and you use the money to buy new assets during the marriage then the new asset becomes matrimonial property.

The basic idea is that a couple should share fairly the net value what is around at the date of separation which has been acquired from their efforts during the marriage. Anything acquired after the separation is not included as matrimonial or partnership property. The values of pension interests and policies which accumulated during the period of the marriage or civil partnership to the date of separation are specifically included as matrimonial or partnership property.

The default is that fair sharing will usually be achieved by equal sharing of the net assets. The division doesn't have to involve splitting each asset. It can be done that way, which might involve pension sharing and selling a family home so each of you receives a share of the proceeds. Another approach is to offset values so that for example one of you keeps a pension and the other the family home.

You might find a mixture of the two approaches of offsetting or sharing works best. Pension sharing involves the transfer of part or all of a pension fund in one person's name to the other person. The provision can be set out in a

Separation Agreement but the transfer of the pension credit from one name to another only takes place after divorce.

The rules also recognise that there can be some circumstances where fairness will not be achieved by equal sharing. Any departure from equal sharing is discretionary and there is no formula to use. The two most commons reasons for unequal sharing are where assets acquired during the marriage derived from funds which would otherwise not have been matrimonial property ('source of funds') or where one person is coming out financially worse off than the other in a way that equal sharing of the assets won't balance out fairly (financial advantage/disadvantage)

If one of you earns significantly more than the other there might be an adjustment either as regular support (periodical allowance) or as a lump sum. Regular support is most usually justified to allow adjustment from depending on your partner's income and can be for up to three years for that reason. It is usually for a shorter time. There are some circumstances where support for a former partner could be for longer than three years.

Neither support for a spouse or civil partner during marriage (aliment) nor periodical allowance for an ex after divorce is taxed if you receive it or gives you tax relief if you pay it. The same goes for child support.

Support for children is often set out in the formal Agreement but now usually follows the formula set out by the statutory Agency which would set the level if it is disputed, the Child Maintenance Service.

Grounds for divorce/ending a Civil Partnership

Although the rules for financial provision are on a 'no fault' basis you can still ask for a divorce based on unreasonable behaviour or adultery. When things are agreed, most people base their divorces on separation for one year with the consent of the other person or two year separation without the need for consent. A Civil Partnership cannot be ended on the basis of adultery but otherwise the same rules apply.

Cohabitation

In Scotland there are potential claims where couples, who have lived together as if married, separate. You have to make a formal claim before the first anniversary of the separation. There is no assumption of equal sharing so the position is very different from married couples. The person making the claim has to establish they are financially disadvantaged at the end of the relationship or will have costs in relation to caring for the children of the relationship in the future (other than those covered by maintenance)

Children

For most separating couples the real priority is for your children not to be damaged by the separation. The trouble is that it can be difficult in the emotional turmoil to separate out the children's perspective from the adult one. The legal rules are clear that the courts should only become involved as a last resort and where decisions have to be made by the courts, they will be driven by the interests of the children. Children's views will be taken into account and the views of children aged 12 and over have particular weight.

Although parents who have been married have the same standing in law when it comes to important decisions, there is no assumption that children's time must be shared between parents. If the division of time has to be decided by a court the orders are for residence or contact. If there are particular matters to be decided such as what school a child should go to or about health then a specific issue order can be requested.

Unmarried fathers have the same rights and responsibilities as married fathers if they are registered on their child's birth certificate on or after 4th May 2006. Otherwise unmarried fathers have no automatic rights but do have the responsibility to support their child financially unless both parents register a form agreeing for the father to have parental rights and responsibilities or the father obtains a court order.

Protective orders

There are a variety of protective orders the Courts can make if there is risk of physical, psychological or financial harm. They can be requested as part of a divorce action or in a separate application to the Court.

Sorting things out

Couples who separate have a range of ways of sorting things out: mediation, Collaborative Practice, lawyer led negotiation, arbitration or litigation. The last two routes involve decisions by a third party. That can be necessary if there is a history of financial dishonesty or physical or emotional abuse.

The ending of a relationship often involves what one of you feels is a breach of trust and in all cases it represents the loss of your hopes in how things would turn out. It can be difficult to contemplate sitting down together to make plans. The complication is that where there are children, the reality is that there will have to be some co-operation down the years.

Using a co-operative process to make the big plans can provide a resilient platform for all the other issues which are likely to come up in the years to come. In Collaborative Practice professionals from a counselling and financial background can work with your lawyer and the other lawyer involved in a very supportive and integrated way.

Resources

Counselling and non-lawyer mediation is available through Relationships Scotland.
www.relationships-scotland.org.uk.
Lawyer mediators can be located through CALM www.calmscotland.co.uk. Professionals from a legal, counselling and financial background who work together in the Collaborative Process can be found through Consensus www.consensus-scotland.com. . Arbitrators from a family law background have an organisation called Family Law Arbitration Scotland (FLAGS) www.flagscotland.com

Lawyers who have an interest in Family Law can be found through the Family Law Association (FLA) www.familylawassociation.org. Some general information and more resources can be found through Right Kind of Divorce www.therightkindofdivorce.com.

I hope this information might help you find the right kind of divorce for you and your family.

Anne Hall Dick, Solicitor, Family Law Matters Scotland.

Family Law Specialist and Family Law Mediator. Trained in Collaborative Practice. Member of FLAGS (Family Law Arbitration Group Scotland)

Family Law Matters Scotland LLP

63 Carlton Place, Glasgow, G5 9TW Tel: 0141 420 2430 www.familylawmattersscotland.co.uk

I am a Partner and family law solicitor at Family Law Matters Scotland in Glasgow.

I have specialised in Family Law for nearly 40 years and I am well known for my writing and training in both in Scotland and elsewhere. I annotate "The Family Law (Scotland) Act 1985" for W Green and co-authored with Tom Ballantine "The Art of Family Law" and "The Science of Family Law". I am also the author of "Child Centred Legal Practice" and wrote a practical guide for individuals going through separation called "Breaking Up - Without Falling Apart!".

I am accredited by the Law Society of Scotland as a specialist in Family law and as a Family Law Mediator. I can help separating couples tackle child and financial issues using mediation. After training in Collaborative Family Law in London, I became one of the original four founder members of the organisation for Collaborative practitioners in Scotland, Consensus, for whom I am Training Convenor. I am an Associate Member of the Chartered Institute of Arbitrators and a committee member of FLAGS, the Family Law Arbitration Group (Scotland).

I was the founder Chairman of the Family Law Association in 1989 and the first Convenor of CALM, the association of Accredited Family Mediators in Scotland.

I have extensive experience of dealing with high value financial cases using either collaborative practice or, where that is not appropriate, in the Court of Session, working with experienced experts. I have conducted several cases in the Sheriff Court in various parts of Scotland dealing with possible relocation of children when one of both parents plan to leave Scotland.

I recognise that the process separating couples use to sort things out will influence what kind of post separation family they have and I am very keen to help that transition be as constructive as possible in the particular circumstances.

Anne Hall Dick
Partner
Family Law Specialist and Family Law Mediator
Trained in Collaborative Practice
Member of FLAGS (Family Law Arbitration Group Scotland)
Family Law Matters Scotland LLP
63 Carlton Place, Glasgow, G5 9TW Tel: 0141 420 2430 www.familylawmattersscotland.co.uk

www.familylawmattersscotland.co.uk
www.therightkindofdivorce.com

18

Divorce around the World

Divorce in the EU

The individual EU countries have their own laws regarding divorce, custody, maintenance and child support. The EU's job is to make sure when people divorce in one country, it is recognized in another. When there is a question regarding which country to divorce in, the EU decides who has jurisdiction to hear the case. Some nationals living in another country may want the divorce where they are living. When spouses are from different countries, the EU settles the matter of where to divorce. The divorce decree from one country is enforced in the other EU countries.

The 2007 Hague Convention set up guidelines for collecting maintenance and child support from EU member countries. Members each have a Central Authority which assists people with applications, enforcement, and modification to maintenance or child support. The Central Authorities work in collaboration with each other in enforcing the divorce decrees. In cases of parental child abduction, the EU countries work together for the child's safe return.

Divorce in New Zealand

New Zealand has a single ground for divorce, the marriage has irreconcilably has broken down. The parties must be unable to reconcile and not have co-habituated for two years. This no fault divorce can be initiated by one party or done together as a joint application. It is filed with the Registrar of the Family Court. Neither party has to attend if uncontested. If the person filing for divorce wants to appear before a judge, or if the divorce is contested, then both parties have to go to court. In the case of a joint filing, the Registrar looks over the papers and can grant a dissolution (divorce) order in six weeks. When one spouse files for divorce, the papers have to be personally handed to the other spouse by someone else. After these papers are received then the spouse who sent them, fills out Affidavit of Service guaranteeing that they were delivered. The other spouse has three weeks to respond. If the spouse who received the divorce papers does not respond, then the Registrar is still able to grant the divorce order.

Australian Divorce

Australia has No-Fault Divorce and the ground is that the marriage has broken down irretrievably. Separation for twelve months and a day is required for the couple, even if it is in the same residence. At least one spouse must be a citizen or have lived in Australia for a year before filing. Spouses must have been married for two years, although in rare cases this may be waived.

The spouses may file a joint application together for the divorce as joint applicants. When only one spouse files, it is as the sole applicant and the other is the respondent. The respondent is served the papers at least twenty-eight days before a court hearing and in turn has the same amount of time to file a Response to Divorce if any inaccuracies are spotted. The sole applicant with a child under eighteen must attend a court hearing, but the respondent is not required to, unless in disagreement with the divorce application and has filed a Response to Divorce. In Australia, spousal maintenance may be provided for a specific time limit, or given as a lump sum when assets are sold in the divorce.

Parents make arrangements for their children in the Parenting Plan. Both parents sign it and a family law attorney then makes it a Consent Order. This Consent Order is binding and enforceable by the court. If the parents are unable to agree upon a Parenting Plan, they are mandated to meet with a child custody mediator to try to reach an agreement. If they are still unable to come to terms regarding the children's arrangements with the mediator's professional guidance, then an application is made to the Family Law Courts for Parenting Orders. There is an interim hearing and input given is provided by a psychologist and witnesses. The children are consulted and a judge makes a determination at the final hearing.

Canadian Divorce

Spouses must remain married for two years before pursuing a divorce, except in rare cases. There is no legal separation in Canada. The main ground for divorce in Canada is separation for one year, whether this takes place in different locations or in separate areas in the marital home. Spouses can be living under the same roof, but consider themselves in separation. The other two grounds are cruelty or adultery, these can be harder to prove, so are used less often. At least one spouse must have lived in

Canada for a year, whether or not they were married in Canada.

The value of the assets – not the actual assets themselves - is divided during the divorce. The assets are valued at the date of separation, except for the marital home. If one spouse receives a big pay bonus during the divorce process, it would be theirs alone, since the assets at the date of separation are valued and divided and this was not part of those. If one spouse has a higher net family property then he must pay the spouse an equalization payment, which is half of both spouses' net family properties. For example, if the husband has a Lamborghini car and expensive items and the wife has an old Ford and small trinkets, she could get an equalization payment. If the husband's net family property is valued and $200,000 and the wife's at $100,000, then half of the difference is $50,000. They would each have $150,000 in valued assets after the wife received the $50,000 equalization payment.

Mediation and collaborative are two ways to get divorced in Canada. If one wants to go through the court, then the spouse files an application for divorce, stating what she wants, such as child support. A financial statement would be filed with this application. A court file is opened and these papers are sent to the other spouse by a process server, or to his attorney. The spouse files a sworn affidavit with the court that her spouse has been served with the papers. The other spouse has thirty days to reply either agreeing or disagreeing with the papers. If your spouse has filed a claim against you, then you have ten days to reply.

A case conference is held to discuss issues, such as arrangements for the children. The law requires both spouses share financial information. A motion is made for an issue that cannot wait until the divorce decree. Obtaining interim child support would be a reason for a motion. In a settlement conference the judge hears both sides, studies the financial records and considers the children's arrangements. He states how he would rule on the case if it were a trial. The judge is attempting to help the spouses come to an agreement so that the case does not go to trial. If the spouses cannot come to terms, then the case goes on to trial. Witnesses are called and documents are presented. At the end of the trial, the judge is not required to make an immediate ruling, so more time may elapse before the divorce is completed.

Child support is not taxable to the parent who receives it, nor is it a deduction for the payer. Alimony is a tax deduction for the payer and is taxed as income for the receiver. There is not a strict formula for alimony, but rather factor such as age and health are taken into consideration.

Mexican Divorces

Mexico at one time was the capital of quick divorces, but this is no longer true. Like the US, Mexico is made up of individual states, so the requirements differ. Mexico requires habitual residency or domicile as do other countries, before granting a divorce. One spouse must be a legal resident for at least six months before starting a divorce. A certificate must be obtained that confirms that you met the legal requirements for divorce. After this, it takes at least three months to divorce. Mexican nationals wanting to divorce in the U.S. could affect their immigration status, so checking with an attorney first is prudent.

19

Self-Medicating

Enjoying a margarita with the girls, or having a pint with mates at the pub is not self-medicating. Drinking because one cannot deal with the pain of life's problems is. Be careful to take prescription medication only as directed and do not mix it with alcohol.

In the therapy world, smoking is sometimes referred to as "slow suicide." In hypnotherapy classes, we were instructed to help move clients towards living a healthy, worthwhile life and away from wanting this slow suicide. Remember, you are modelling behaviour for your children.

It is not worth giving your spouse ammunition in a custody battle, by drinking or taking drugs. You do not know when a surprise drug test may be ordered by the court, if there are rumours of usage. You are teaching your children a crucial life skill when you deal with your problems in a constructive manner.

Cathy was happily married, with a young daughter, and building a dream house with her husband. They regularly entertained, rode horses, did community service and had a great life. Cathy had overcome a drinking problem in the past and was a fragile person who felt life's blows acutely. Her husband took some business trips out of state and met a married woman in his line of work. This woman previously had an affair, then divorced her husband to marry her lover. Cathy received a phone call from the other woman's husband when their spouses were having an affair. Cathy could not cope and began a downward spiral with alcohol. Cathy's husband divorced her and married the other woman, who moved into the dream house. The couple deviously campaigned to obtain full custody of the daughter and were successful, partly due to Cathy's increased drinking. Cathy's parents helped tremendously, but she still had a breakdown and was put on medication. This drama continued, culminating when the new wife refused to let the daughter call her mother on Mother's Day. By now the daughter was older and possibly could have called her mother surreptitiously. A few days later, Cathy took an unintentional overdose of prescription medication, compounded by alcohol, and died.

Self-medicating to alleviate the emotional pain of divorce does not eliminate the trauma, it only temporarily numbs it. It postpones dealing with it in a constructive way that will lead to permanent, long-lasting results. It does not allow you to deeply process and release these emotions. They stay trapped in your body and may explode in a destructive way. Taking illicit drugs, alcohol or too much prescription medication is detrimental to your body, spirit and to those around you. Some people who have used alcohol as a crutch described this period as living in a haze. After going to AA, they said that memories were still a blur from that time period. Be fully present in your kids' lives and cherish those childhood recollections.

Problem: What to do in the turmoil of divorce when alcohol is calling out your name too frequently

Solution: Discovering a passion or long lost hobby can be the antidote to the temptation of self-medication. One fellow said that gardening is a great way to forget about divorce and to centre himself. His plants depend upon his care plus give a purpose and focus to his daily routine. His reward is beautiful blooms and organic vegetables.

Having someone else (person, animal, plants) depend upon you can be the motivating factor to walk away from an addiction. In the book by James Bowen, *A Street Cat Named Bob*, the author pens his true story how taking in a stray orange cat turns his life around. He leaves his drug abuse behind in order to create a better existence for them both.

One woman leaves the house for a run or lattes with the girls, when alcohol is a temptation. She would rather get pampered than suffer through a hangover the following morning. Others enjoy subscribing to a web site that sends them positive quotes and exquisite photos of nature. High quality chocolate is my particular vice. If too many bottles of wine are calling out your name, then seek out a medical professional.

20

Using Supplements in Divorce

Homeopathic Remedies

There are great brands of homeopathic remedies to address the moods and emotions that come with divorce. Some like Boiron and Bach's Flower Remedies have been around for decades and others are the new kids on the block with a developing base of fans. Since emotions influence our health and well-being, these homeopathies are worth checking out.

People have shared stories of how Bach Flower Remedies have made a difference in their lives. Dr. Bach was a physician (1886–1936) who had the modern thinking that "Our fears, our cares, our anxieties, and things like that, open the path to the invasion of illness." Dr. Bach utilized different flower essence combinations to get rid of mental and emotional stress. Current research has shown the link between stress and/or anger in bringing on heart attacks and strokes. These flower remedies are helpful in preventing a condition or disease. The remedies are also specific to certain anxieties.

For long term use during my divorce, I used Walnut, which is for a change in your life, such as a divorce, move, new job or loss of someone. "The remedy gives constancy and protection from outside influences." It really did its job and I felt calmer and more in control during my divorce. I used this daily. One mother uses Walnut to help her deal with her son's divorce and said she feels more relaxed about it now.

Rescue Remedy is quick acting and used in acute situations, such as a court hearing. I literally used three to four drops a few minutes before I walked in the door for my collaborative divorce sessions. A few times, I excused myself during the middle and popped a few more drops in my mouth. Post-divorce, when we had a court hearing, Rescue Remedy was invaluable. I keep SLEEP Rescue Remedy in my nightstand and do three squirts if I wake up in the middle of the night.

White Chestnut is for those who cannot stop persistent thoughts, ideas or arguments entering their minds, making sleep and concentration more difficult. I am using this one now, post-divorce and find it easier to drift off to dreamland. A student getting her Master's Degree also finds it beneficial in quieting her mind at night.

Olive is for those who have suffered much mentally or physically and feel that they have no more strength to deal with daily life. This one may be helpful for people coming out of an abusive marriage. Willow is for those who suffered great adversity and feel that it was unfair. They are embittered and lose interest in previously enjoyable pursuits. This one is particularly helpful for those embroiled in an acrimonious divorce, who may not see the light at the end of the tunnel.

The above information can be found online or at the display area surrounding the bottles of Bach Flower Remedies in natural grocers and herbalists. I also like Boiron for emotional issues and physical symptoms. As a Nurse, I recommend Boiron's great ones for sinus pain, allergies, colds, and the flu. A naturopath can offer assistance with choosing the best remedies for you.

Dr. Bach said that the thymus is particularly affected by the emotions of hate and envy. An under active-thymus depresses the immune system. Dr. Bach said that illness is "Disharmony and imbalance...between the soul and the mind."

What Supplements to Take?

Getting through a divorce can be traumatic. This stress can have detrimental effects on the body, particularly the cardiovascular system. Chronic stress keeps the body on alert that disaster is approaching. Taking supplements can help mitigate this situation.

Studies indicate that Omega-3 protects the heart by maintaining an optimal rhythm and by increasing blood vessel flexibility. It decreases inflammation in the body. *The Journal of Psychiatry* is studying the use of Omega-3 for people with depression and other mental disorders. An Ohio State University study indicated that it decreases mild anxiety. Medical students participated for a twelve week period, with one group taking Omega-3 and the other a placebo. The results showed a 20% decrease in anxiety with the Omega-3 group and a 14% decrease in the pro-inflammatory compound, interleukin 6.

Interleukin 6 is an anti-inflammatory when it is within normal limits. It relays information between cells, regulates cell growth and the immune system functioning. It helps to stop colds and infections. Psychological stress causes inflammation in the body and this in turn elevates interleukin 6 into the pro-inflammation range. When this happens, it can lead to diseases such as autoimmune disorders including rheumatoid arthritis.

Another study advocates Omega-3 for kids with asthma, and my son was able to permanently get off an asthma medicine with regular usage. Remember, a good portion of your brain is made up of healthy fat, so the healthy fats in Omega-3 are useful for brain functioning and memory.

Another important supplement for stress is Holy Basil, which decreases cortisol levels. Cortisol is a stress hormone which causes increased heart rate, blood pressure and insomnia. Cortisol is responsible for the "flight or fight" response. In Indian Ayurvedic medicine, Holy Basil also has anti-mutagenic, and anti-inflammatory properties. It has been prescribed for several millenniums in India. This helped me to relax better and get to sleep quicker during my divorce, and I continued the next year to take this fantastic supplement post-divorce. My son is in college, works two jobs, and depends upon Holy Basil to get him through this hectic time.

High cortisol levels can cause headaches and aroma therapists often recommend Clary Sage essential oil to reduce this pain and relax muscles in the cranial-sacral areas. Lavender has a soothing effect on anxiety and comes in many forms, such as a facial spray or in a small bottle to roll on your temples and wrists. Scientists at Stanford University suggest calming the central nervous system by inhaling the fragrance of tangerine. Aromatherapy helped me in divorce and afterwards. Neal's Yard skin care has aromatic essential oils that soothes tension and anxiety away. Having a facial there in London is my ultimate bliss.

Bee pollen has vitamins, amino acids, trace minerals and enzymes. Milk thistle helps to promote healthy liver functioning and detoxification. This is particularly good if you have been eating more junk food, or have a glass too many with friends.

When your body in under the stress of divorce, B Vitamins are depleted. B6 is especially important for immune health. When an individual's B6 level is low, then the production of White Blood Cells, T Cells, and interleukin 2 are decreased. These elements are needed to fight off colds and infections. B12 is required for cell growth and division, and is naturally decreased in middle age and under stress. You may want to consider having your B level tested, particularly for B12. Biotin is needed for the production of insulin and aids in the metabolism of glucose, fatty acids, and amino acids. Consider taking a multi B vitamin complex in when under the duress of divorce. When I am lax taking B complex, I tend to have more headaches.

Lecithin granules contain phospholipids and help the brain in learning. I also take it for its aid in nerve functioning, since phospholipids are found in the brain tissue.

Co Enzyme Q10 is an element found in the mitochondria of cells, particularly those in the heart. It converts food into energy and diminishes free radicals. A study at Tulane University in New Orleans indicated that Co Q10 increased the ejection fraction (pumping ability of the heart) by 3.7%. Skin care companies have added Q10 into their wide ranges of beauty products. I take it every day to promote healthy heart functioning.

Bilberry contains antioxidants that fight free radicals. It increases strength and flexibility of capillary walls for micro circulation. Capillaries have a small diameter so keeping walls flexible promotes good blood flow to carry nutrients throughout the body. It is also associated with eye health since they contain a lot capillaries. Various studies on Bilberry indicate that it also strengthens the collagen in arterial walls which helps to decrease clot formation. Stress is particularly detrimental to the cardiovascular system, so I included these supplements into my daily regime.

Antioxidants have gotten a lot of press recently, but what are they? These nutrients, including flavonoids, decrease free radicals. Free radicals are the waste material of cells that increase inflammation in the body. Another function of some antioxidants is to deter these inflammatory elements from sticking to healthy cells. Berries and tea are good sources of antioxidants and I enjoy the calming effect of tea.

Biochemical Pharmacology had an article that stated Curcumin (from turmeric) decreased inflammation in ninety-seven or more "biological mechanisms." One is decreasing interleukin 6 which causes inflammation. Curcumin has been has been used in Ayurvedic healing for a few millenniums, particularly for gastro-intestinal problems.

Some busy parents have commented that they and the kids do not consume enough green veggies. While it is preferable to eat more green vegetables, drinking them will do. There are several green powders that you can mix with water to fill this nutritional gap. Green Edge Powder or Perfect Green are two examples that contain all sorts of vegetables, grasses, seeds and seaweed to give your family a nutritional boost.

If you are not a breakfast person, or need a quick nutritional boost before leaving the house, here is a tip. Consume a protein powder mixed with milk, such as Spiru-tein. It contains trace elements, amino acids, chlorophyll, enzymes, apple pectin, vitamins and minerals.

Verify whether your supplements have a single ingredient or are combinations. My Omega-3 is just that, but other brands have Resveratrol in them. Some Q10 capsules also contain Omega-3, listed in smaller print. You do not want to double up on some of these supplements by accident, so check the labels carefully.

Stress and strong emotions can wreak havoc with your bowel functioning. A GI doctor gave me this tip: Take psyllium to regulate your GI tract, whether having diarrhoea or constipation. For diarrhoea, psyllium bulks up the stool, and for constipation, it helps you become more regular. Metamucil contains psyllium. I buy psyllium for less than a brand name one at Trader Joe's grocery store and it does not have additives. Check with your healthcare provider before adding supplements to your diet.

21

Therapy

Therapy helps you develop greater insight on various situations and handle relationships better. Therapy cannot make you instantly happy, but it can illuminate a path that leads you to have an easier time in life. Lucy Beresford states, in UK's *Psychologies Magazine*, that "Therapy won't work miracles, but it can do many other things. It can boost self-esteem, untangle emotional dilemmas, provide support during grief or trauma, and facilitate the discovery of courage to face the world again after illness, divorce." A therapist can help someone who feels stuck in her life or at a crossroads, by enabling her to sort things out and get motivated for change.

When someone feels overwhelmed with time management issues or keeping their head above water during divorce, then this may be more in the realm of a life coach. Some life coaches specialize in the area of divorce and can help one to get their life back on track when stuck on an issue. This is short-term and may be limited to one or two areas. If someone feels unsure about what their life purpose is, a coach helps them to define goals and formulate a plan on how to reach them. Life coaching works in the present and future, while therapy can delve into the past to determine how that influences the client's functioning now.

Types of Therapy

Some people wonder what type of questions they will be asked by a therapist. That depends upon the type of therapy your psychologist practices. For example, psychoanalysis is an intensive type of therapy that can take years. The goal is for a client to gain insight regarding her problems and the source of these detrimental behaviours, in order for change to occur. A therapist that does cognitive behaviour therapy gives more advice and helps clients change thought patterns and expectations. Cognitive therapy is more concrete and works well with phobias, addictions and obsessive compulsive disorder. The cognitive psychologist may give an estimate for a specific number of sessions, since this is a much shorter type of therapy.

Humanistic therapy deals with your individual development as a person, rather than on a mental disorder. These therapists feel that events, such as abuse in childhood, interrupt the person's development, and they work with the client to fix the developmental process.

You do not have to tell your therapist your deepest, darkest secrets, but not doing so can impede your progress in therapy. What you withhold may be the crucial piece of information that needs to be addressed to improve your well-being. Some people are afraid they may become too dependent upon the therapist or even develop romantic feelings towards them. Transference is when you view your therapist as more of a parent or partner. It may be embarrassing, but bring it up, because this can happen in therapy, and therapists are especially trained on how to deal with this issue. Your therapist can work with the concept of transference to enable your other relationships to be more meaningful.

Often, at the beginning of therapy, your therapist will discuss how many sessions that he thinks you will need. Of course, this can be adjusted if you sail through and feel you have met your goals early. If more complex issues arise, then the amount of sessions will lengthen. Ultimately, you have the final say on when to stop the sessions. Success will be judged by noticing a difference in how you think and handle situations. This can be a very gradual process.

Group therapy is especially effective when it centres around a specific issue, such as grief or addictions. The other group members can help each other gain clarity and see that they are not the only one in that situation. The group leader may or may not be a psychologist. What is said in group therapy does not leave the room.

Hypnosis is one of the three natural altered states of the mind, with the other two being meditation and prayer. In hypnosis, the barrier between the conscious and subconscious minds opens. The subconscious is more receptive to suggestions for change and will only accept directions that are in your belief system. If you are against theft, then in hypnosis your subconscious mind would not accept the suggestion to embezzle or rob a bank. The subconscious mind runs the autonomic nervous system, so that is why hypnosis is such a valuable agent to instigate bodily change. The autonomic nervous system regulates breathing, blood pressure, heart rate, metabolism, cell changes, and so forth. Hypnotherapy helps with a plethora of conditions, such as insomnia, weight control, back pain, smoking cessation, anxiety, plus much more. Hypnotherapy delves back to the root of the problem and deals with the surrounding emotions, in order to release them, thereby promoting healing.

The subconscious mind is very literal. If your basic needs were not met as small child, it may conclude that you are "not worthy." This feeling of being "not worthy" can run your life, driving you to seek out people and situations that validate that you are "not worthy." Hypnosis is invaluable in changing these faulty self-beliefs, and can sometimes make huge changes in only one session.

Children in Therapy

Sometimes a child does not adapt well to divorce or the visitation transitions, so may go into therapy. PTSD is one reason that was mentioned in an earlier chapter. One elementary school child had an insane visitation schedule that was solely for the parents. Every night he went to the other parent's house and soon developed an eating disorder. I was a nurse to a high school student of divorce, who also developed an eating disorder and was hospitalized for several months. An eating disorder is a way to gain control over oneself when the rest of your life is in chaos.

Depression can be a by-product of divorce which needs to be treated. We had a few kids at my schools who were molested and were making progress moving on with their lives while seeing a therapist. When one parent has impairment issues that affects the child's well-being and social services monitors this situation.

Children can develop attention seeking behaviours or are disruptive, so are referred to the school counsellor. She may then recommend private therapy.

Therapy is a great opportunity for children to express their sadness or anger regarding their uprooted lives from divorce. The neutral therapist and children come up with strategies to help them adjust to this new situation in a healthier way.

22

Holiday Season

"I used to think the worst thing in life was to end up alone, it's not. The worst thing in life is to end up with people that make you feel all alone."
—Robin Williams

Christmas and New Year's Celebrations

Here are some tips on surviving Christmas and other holidays without your kids while in a divorce situation. Even if you do not have any children, your holidays will be quite different during and post-divorce. I got some wonderful British magazines, such as *Woman and Home*, *Good Housekeeping UK* and *Red* as a present to myself. After we had a lovely Christmas morning at home, my two sons left with their father. I had uninterrupted time, which I spent drinking tea and reading these cheery magazines. I sat near the Christmas tree with my cats, and the afternoon without my kids flew by comfortably.

My mother's tip is to work on Christmas. She worked in a hospital and then a nursing home, both being festive places with yummy food and parties. My mother liked my stepmother, so she knew that I was having fun with her family on holidays when I was there during visitation.

There are a plethora of charities that especially need help over the holidays. In the UK, Contact the Elderly, has monthly get-togethers for elderly people living alone. Their Christmas parties are extra festive, with carols, presents, yummy food and sherry. Some volunteers have formed closed bonds with the aged person assigned to them, and also claim to get a tremendous personal benefit from helping out with this charity. You may want to see what volunteer options are available in your area.

Some people get a lot of satisfaction helping out at a homeless shelter on Thanksgiving and Christmas. Animals at shelters or rescue groups still need to eat and have litter boxes changed. My older son seems to have to do this duty on holidays for his cat rescue group.

Do you have any single friends who get together on holidays? After being married for so long, you may not know what they do at Christmas time or Thanksgiving. What do your other divorced friends do on holidays? Maybe you could all rent a chick flick and have a little spiked nog to increase your holiday spirit. If your family lives nearby, spend time with them.

Be glad that you do not have to go to all those time-consuming holiday cocktail parties now, as you did when still married. Just think of the fun things you can do with the kids post-divorce with that extra time. Make a gingerbread house from a kit, bake festive cookies for gifts, eat pizza in PJs and watch "Elf" or "White Christmas."

One divorced friend got me spa products for Christmas so I could pamper myself in peace when my boys went to their father's house. Another newly divorced friend got a best-seller and waited until the kids went to their other parent's house, to dive into the book.

If you have shared custody, when your children will be away for a week or two, go out of town. Friends who have been to the European Christmas markets rave about these trips. Go on a Viking River Cruise in Germany and you will be around many other people during this festive time. My sons and I finally went on one this past year and enjoyed mixing with other folks. It was invigorating wandering around the brightly lit markets while sipping hot drinks. The ship had a German children's choir on board and another night Slovakian/Hungarian folkloric dancers.

When you are alone on a ship, you are far more likely to reach out to other people and make new friends. As a new divorcee, Kim went on a Cunard Line ship for a Christmas cruise and enjoyed the festivities, holiday shows, food, plus being with the other passengers. It was fun for her to attend a big, black tie bash for New Year's Eve and not need a date. My sons and I went on a Holland America ship for Christmas around New Zealand and a little of Australia. We dumped our pre-divorce holiday rituals for new ones post-divorce on this journey.

Decide if you want to be a hermit or dance the night away on New Year's Eve to celebrate your new found freedom post-divorce. Some newly divorced people have shied away from small, intimate gatherings with many couples and have gone for the big galas instead, where conversation can be more superficial. One aspect of New Year's Eve is that couples may be together and less inclined to invite single pals along to party with them. I felt lonelier while still married on New Year's Eve, than I ever did post-divorce. I then celebrated it with my mother and sons, eating luscious treats while watching the ball drop in Times Square. One can earn a bit of cash babysitting on this holiday. Now New Year's Eve is quiet and my sons celebrate New Year's Day with me.

The Washington Post had an article that said 49% of adults over 18 are not married (but some may be in relationships). In the UK, from 2001 to 2011, one person households increased by half a million. This is a large number of people not joined at the hip with a spouse on New Year's Eve. Now increasing numbers of singles are celebrating this two-day holiday, which ups your chance of spending it with unattached friends. Whatever you decide to do New Year's Eve and Day, remember to take the supplement Milk Thistle to support your liver with the extra alcohol consumption.

Thanksgiving

Start new family traditions, after getting input from your children on what they especially would like to do. Mix the old traditions with new ones. We have a nice brunch at home on Thanksgiving Day, while watching the Macy's parade. Then it is off to a movie, followed by a simple pot roast dinner at home later. We used to go to an over-priced restaurant on Thanksgiving, but now enjoy our new tradition much better.

See if there is a single's group in your town or church that may be getting together on this day. My local MeetUp.com group meets at a fun restaurant for a Thanksgiving Day luncheon. This is a good way to be social when does not have the time or cash to fly across the country to be with family. Shake up your former routine by having a breakfast feast at a café and then veg out in front of the TV. You can do your regular rituals, perhaps in a different order. Pick up a delectable treat the day before, if you are planning on staying home.

Valentine's Day

Valentine's Day can be especially challenging for those newly single when it seems like everyone else is paired like Noah's Ark. Decide if you want to treat it as a non-event or stay at home, avoiding it altogether. I was doing a radio interview on February 15th in Chicago and arrived early on

Valentine's Day. Due to a snow storm, my college pal was unable to drive there to spend a girls' weekend with me post-divorce. What to do solo? I wandered around and stumbled upon a department store doing facials and makeovers. The cosmetician was also divorced, and we had a great conversation. I felt wonderful and liked the new, more polished me after Valerie worked her magic. Grabbing a gourmet chocolate on the way out was pampering as well. The full moon shimmered on the ice-covered river, and many were taking photos. Topping the evening off at a tea room reading and people-watching made an enjoyable Valentine's night. Be open to new experiences that can turn your world around. What started out as disappointing changed into a fun St. Valentine's Day.

Some friends enjoy having children around on this day as a happy distraction post-divorce. They stated that it is more difficult to feel sorry for themselves when busy entertaining kids. Endear yourself with friends by offering to babysit on Valentine's night, Invite nieces and nephews over for a Disney marathon.

Benny started going to an upscale natural grocery store on holidays after his break up. They have gourmet food that can be eaten at the communal table and washed down with lattes. He enjoys the camaraderie and says it is like a party.

Consider meeting pals earlier in the day for lattes or lunch. Get something decadent to eat at home later. You still get out on the day, but are not around romantic couples in the evening.

Completing challenges that you never thought possible is a big boost for self-esteem. There are charity organizations that have treks and cycling trips around the planet over Valentine's Day. Some examples are a trek up Mt. Kilimanjaro, and Charity Challenge has had a cycling trip from Saigon to Angkor Wat. There is a plethora of possibilities, such as going to the Rift Valley, Morocco, and hiking the Inca Trail. One gets pledges, and doing these life changing experiences also earns money for various charities. Do an online search for charity treks.

Outward Bound has programs that are sometimes over Valentine's Day. They may be hikes, mountain climbing or other outdoor pursuits which lead to personal growth. Their motto is participants "emerge to find out that they can do more than they thought they could."

Time does help heal a broken heart, and Valentine's Day does get easier down the road. The key to surviving holidays on your own is distraction, whether watching a movie, reading a great book, or catching up with pals. Take your mind off your newly divorced status and do something enjoyable.

23

Cutting Costs and Gaining Money

Money may be needed quickly during divorce for your lawyer's retainer and living expenses. There are some quick, but legal ways to raise cash in a hurry.

When my husband left me, I lost my job and had no income for over a month, while the interim support was being determined. The bills still needed to be paid, so I had to discover ways to obtain instant cash from my belongings. My sons helped with thinking up ways to slash spending. I still had to give gifts and buy food, personal care products and so forth. I bought a house during my divorce, and required a chunk of cash for the down payment.

Money from Your Possessions

If you have an overabundance of family heirlooms, consider asking family members if they would like a great deal on them. Your sister may have been coveting Gran's china that you can easily live without. You get cash and family members get cherished wares.

Check your jewellery box and other places around your house for broken chains, old class rings and jewellery which you no longer like or wear. You may find some beat up sterling silverware and utensils. Take them to your local metal/coin shop to get instant cash. Local coin shops want your repeat business, and I found mine to be honest and fair. I have heard mixed reviews about the places where you mail in your jewellery or companies coming to town for one day to purchase your goods. Old family pieces, which are tarnished or just 10 karat gold, can also be sold. If the item is gold or silver-plated, then it is not accepted at my local metal shop.

Go to your local consignment store to sell higher quality jewellery. Some may buy your pieces outright. You would be surprised what your vintage broach will fetch. Unique or antique jewellery boxes can do well also. Polish your jewellery and silver items before taking them to a consignment shop.

Another avenue is to sell your jewellery online. Brand names do better than generic pieces, because buyers often look up items by brands, such as Tiffany or H. Samuel. If you do not want to do online sales yourself, then take them to a local business that puts items online for a percentage of the sale. I have even gotten decent prices selling my jewellery at garage sales, particularly if I put an ad in the paper stating that I had bracelets and rings to sell. For very unique pieces, some people put an ad in the classifieds with a photograph.

Early editions of some of my childhood books did not sell online, but did at my local used bookstore. Instead of selling extra nice coffee table books or gift-type ones at your garage sale, make a lot more by taking them to a used book dealer. Over the last several years, I have made several hundred dollars extra by doing just this. I have even called the owner of the used bookstore from garage sales and charity shops to see if some books are worth purchasing and selling to him at a small profit. He is very kind about that since we have done a lot of business together.

Look through your old toys and games. I sold a game from my childhood for $65 online and other ones for a little less. My gently used Coach handbags have fetched a modest price. Do an inventory of items that you would like to sell and check their prices online. If you really do love a plate and it is only selling for $15, it is better to keep it. Use the Internet to get an up to the minute guide for pricing, even if you are taking items to a consignment shop.

I had purchased paintings from charity auctions or estate sales for usually up to several hundred dollars. Post-divorce, I doubled or tripled my profit on most of them that I received as an asset.

Slash Household Bills

Tips for saving money around your house. To avoid paying for extra electricity that you're not currently using, unplug appliances, phone chargers and so forth. Many people are unaware that electricity still goes from the wall to your appliance, even when it is turned off. When my coffee maker is turned off, there still is a light on, unless it is unplugged. Tell your kids to unplug the toaster when they are done using it. Check with your utility company to see if the rates are cheaper at certain non-peak times and do your washing then. Put your computer, printer and other gadgets on a power strip with an off switch. Turn it off when not in use, especially at bedtime. I fine my older son a dollar per night if he leaves the power strip on, after being on his computer. So far, I only had to collect this fee once.

Do not automatically turn on a light when you enter a room, such as a bathroom, if you can get enough light through a window to brush your teeth. You will increase the value of your house if you add several sky lights, and you may be eligible for an energy saving tax write off. Good places for these would be in your kitchen or over your bathroom countertop.

In the UK, there are utility companies whose prices vary, so comparative shopping will net the best deal. There are several online sites that compare your particular usage which then shows which utility company has the best rate for your situation. There are programs that offer cash-back deals from selected merchants. In some of these, the money earned from the cash-back purchases can be used to pay utility bills. One woman showed me that she paid £5 for her utilities that month, due to buying a few necessities on the cash-back scheme.

When you are brushing your teeth, turn off the water, unless you are actually rinsing off your toothbrush. My sons scoop up the water from their baths or showers to water plants. Some people collect rain water in barrels and water their gardens from this. These barrels have spigots to which one can attach a hose.

When you buy gas, make sure to get every drop. Do not disconnect the gas hose form your car immediately. Rather, wait a moment and confirm that there are not any drops left. Plot out the route for your errands so that they are bunched together. This way you are not backtracking which saves time and gas. Notice if on a certain day of the week the gas prices change. Ours usually go up on Mondays, so I fill up my tank on Sundays.

A simple way to avoid high plumbing bills is to remove the clogs in drains with "Zip-It." This nifty gadget is a long piece of flexible plastic with small protuberances that grab hair easily. Even unskilled people like me can do it. I bought it at Ace Hardware for less than $10 and it has lasted four years so far. This "Zip-It" saves you from spending money on costly chemicals or natural remedies to unclog those drains.

In the kitchen, get the most out of your trash liners. When you have messy garbage, such as peelings or egg shells, put them inside a container in the trash bin, such as an empty cereal box. This way, you can reuse liners instead of throwing them away each time when you empty the garbage.

Egg shells can go in the dirt for plants, giving them extra nutrients. Used tea leaves buried in the soil of houseplants releases nitrogen. These both save money on buying fertilizer. Buy vegetable broth or a vegetable soup in a box to use as a base, then put any leftover vegetables in this. You can puree this soup, or leave it chunky. One divorced woman planned her grocery shopping at a store around mealtimes. They were generous with samples and she took advantage of this.

Reuse the wax paper bags inside cereal boxes. Shake out any crumbs and use these to put cold cuts in, and to put over opened food in the freezer. These are good to reuse in lunch boxes or when you are sending treats to someone. Utilize tissue paper from boxes and other purchases to wrap Christmas stocking stuffers. Save ribbons and the metallic cords from chocolate boxes to reuse for tiny gifts.

Many libraries have a rack where people leave magazines. I stop by and select some of these free, new issues instead of purchasing them. I often leave mine there or trade magazines with a neighbour. My book club does a book swap for Christmas or we stock up when the library has a used book fair.

Here are a few tips about cleaning for low or no cost. Use a recycled spray bottle with 1/3 bleach to 2/3 water to spray on counters or floors. I use this around the shower and window sills to prevent mildew. Some people prefer to use hydrogen peroxide instead of bleach. After taking a shower, when the mirror is still steamy, take a cloth or paper towel and take advantage of free steam power to wipe off spots from the mirror. When traveling, use the shampoo in the hotel to clean your clothes, without spending money to tote along special fabric wash. My clothes have always done well with this and I avoid expensive laundering charges.

I buy beautiful boxed cards, which are cheaper than individual special occasion ones. I have stampers with "Happy Birthday," "Get Well," "Happy Anniversary," and more. I carefully stamp the message in the middle of the card and sign them. My cards are unique, such as vintage travel posters or Asian paintings, and I paid less than a dollar.

Great Gifts that Won't Blow the Budget

To avoid big January bills, go through your treasure to discover gifts you can give to others who will appreciate them. Family members will enjoy receiving personal legacies. One grandfather gave his grandson part of his coin collection. The father gifted a few of his old coins for the kid's next birthday. A childless aunt passed along her Madame Alexander doll collection to a grateful niece.

A first time mother may treasure her grandmother's first edition children's storybooks or baby china/silver. Round out the gift with an inexpensive new item. People receive so much clothing at baby showers and the infant grows quickly, hardly wearing some outfits for very long. Family heirlooms last.

I gave my son who is majoring in Culinary Arts, his great-grandmother's cookbook with her hand written notes. Also included in that gift was a copy of his preschool class's cookbook that I received as a present one year. A gift card to a local gourmet shop, or exotic spices is a nice added touch.

Homemade goodies at the holidays are especially appreciated by teachers and neighbours. Magazines have great ideas in this department. Charity shops have lovely platters, decorative containers, and plates for a few dollars or pounds, which are a nice addition to one's delectable baked goods.

A great source of presents is your jewellery collection. My aunt likes Native American jewellery, so I gave her a lovely turquoise necklace that I had only worn a couple of times. Small dainty earrings that sit in the bottom of your jewellery box, may be a hit with your young niece. I have given several necklaces that were made from 1930's New Orleans's glass Mardi Gras beads to friends who just loved them, since I had extras to spare. Aim for unique presents at zero cost.

Start drawing names for a Christmas gift exchange, so each kid buys something for one cousin and you are not purchasing many toys for nieces and nephews. Consider having a children only gift exchange. One family could give a group gift to another family, such as the latest board game. The UK store John Lewis, has an employee demonstrating the new and classic games by letting you play along with him. What a fun way to select a family gift. Your family members may want to limit gifts, but do not want to be the one initially bringing up the idea. Inquire how they feel about drawing another's name for a more limited gift exchange. I read how three sisters put a limit of around £10 for each other's birthday gifts. The competition is so fierce, you would think it was a blood sport. The ladies find fabulous gifts on the cheap when traveling, at clearance sales, etc., but all manage to give incredible presents on that budget.

A way to have no debts after Christmas, with holiday gift-giving is using layaway. K-Mart and other stores do layaway as well as some high-end local consignment shops. This way you can start selecting gifts and making your payments in affordable increments in advance. Examine your budget to determine how much you can spend on presents, so that the payments will be completed before Christmas. This enables you to curtail those last minute-impulse purchases and not be bombarded with bills in January.

Churches and schools have one day jumble sales as fundraisers. I found some top of the line toys still in the wrappers which I later sold on e-Bay for a profit. I also purchased some new items in boxes which I gave as presents. These items may have been donated because they are not someone's cup of tea, or may be the contents of a deceased family member's estate. Inspect the clothes selection to see if anything in someone's size still has the tags on it.

Wander into charity shops when traveling, to purchase locally made products at a fraction of the usual cost. Oxfam is a wonderful charity, whose UK shops are treasure troves. In York, England the Oxfam shop had the latest mystery novels which I had just purchased at a bookshop. I did a good bit of shopping at one when on a nurses' conference in St. Andrews, Scotland. It was centrally located and sold locally made vases and other handicrafts, which were brand new.

Look like a Diva on Scrooge's Budget

The best beauty secret costs nothing and it is to have a positive outlook. Some facial lines are caused by the repetitive furrowing of the brow with worries, and others by anger. One bitter relative chronically purses her lips when she is delivering a tirade. Not surprising that she has many lines around her lips. My more angelic friends have smoother skin. Chinese Face reading is based on how temperament and emotions correlate with lines and the structure of the face.

Some great skin products that are at least 1/2 to 2/3 of the department or specialty store price, are the Boots Botanics line, which is from a pharmaceutical store chain originating in the UK. These natural, healthy products are chock full of plant nutrition for the skin and many are certified organic by Kew Gardens in London. Some favourites are: Boots Botanics organic body oil, lotion, skin serum, rose water toner, and their Triple Age Renewal Facial Serum with orchid extract. These low-cost, high-performance products make great gifts. I like Boot's No. 7 line of cosmetics which are cheaper and work better for me than the French brands that I previously used when married.

Friends have tried Burt's Bees products and also rate them highly. Trader Joe's and other grocery stores have some well performing lotions and body oils, packed full of nutrients without preservatives, dyes and other chemicals. Their jojoba body oil is around $7.00, Vitamin E oil is $5 and the body cream is a bargain for around $4. Organic coconut oil is healthy whether you eat it or slather it over your body. This also applies to grape seed oil and these are a bargain in the grocery aisle.

A money saver is to use your favourite brand's body butter, instead of designated hand lotion, with similar results. My body butter is eight ounces and the hand lotion is 1.5 ounces at almost the same price. I purchase a hand lotion only to tote around in my purse or travel bag.

More luxe for less is with Lumene from Finland. It is affordable, containing ingredients such as Arctic cloudberry, cranberry, and Vitamin C. The "Energy Cocktail Intensive Serum" is great first thing in the morning along with their vitamin C facial cream. Medicines and chemicals are absorbed through the skin, so make sure you use high quality products such as the ones mentioned above.

Have baby soft feet using Vermont's "Bag Balm," which has been produced for over 100 years. This ten ounce tin of ointment costs around $9 and a tiny bit is all that is needed to heal dry, cracked heels and wake up with silky skin. This is sold in some drug stores and online. Trader Joe's has a lovely multi-use balm for around four dollars.

Farmer's and Flea markets have natural lotions, lavender sachets and other goodies made with locally grown herbs and plants. Their prices are lower, without having a store's overhead. I have received lovely herbs and other potted plants as gifts which were purchased at these markets. The venders are often willing to negotiate on prices, especially when buying in bulk.

24

Clearing out Your Possessions

Is being tethered to your possessions holding you hostage? Are you staying put because too much stuff is keeping you from moving to a more desirable location? One divorced woman married a man who loved sailing around the world in his boat. Kaitlin had the dilemma of what to do with her life's accumulations, since most of them could not be accommodated on the boat. She culled some of it and put the rest into storage. After sailing for several years, Kaitlin came to the realization that she could live without her possessions as well as her second husband. She donated her belongings and got another divorce. Kaitlin likes the adventure of living in different places, so has moved a few times post-divorce and enlarged her network of friends.

Divorce is an emotionally charged period, and the secret is to calm your mind with meditation, relaxation CDs, or whatever works, so that clear-headed decisions can be made. One may later rue getting rid of special items out of anger or spite. Selling possessions in a panic can cause regrets down the road. I sold a sentimental amber necklace that I bought on a trip with my late mother for only a small sum. I would love to be wearing it now.

This is the time to go through your possessions and see what you can let go. Items that were significant in your marriage enable you to stay attached to your former spouse. The lovely porcelain piece from your honeymoon in France may stir up memories from happier times. Consider selling it to sever this attachment to your ex. I wore the t-shirts that my ex had given me during marriage, on a safari in Africa. This was a nurses' trip and we gathered our gently worn clothes as a donation to an orphanage. Nice way to get rid of gifts from my ex-husband. I sold all of my wedding china and crystal, since keeping them would have been a tie to my ex. I was not going to be giving huge dinner parties after my divorce. I used this money to go on a cruise with my sons and mother. Unfortunately it was her last trip, so I am glad to have replaced material goods with fond memories.

One could give platters to relatives so that they could use them for holiday potlucks. You end up with more space, plus give family members a hint that your holiday cooking will be more limited. If a child is moving away from home soon, pare down your extra household goods that you can live without and place them in a bin for her.

If you kept the marital home in your divorce, then perhaps it is time to donate or sell some items and start anew. Catherine Ponder states in her book, *Open Your Mind to Prosperity*, that to achieve prosperity, "You must get rid of what you don't want to make the way for what you do want." If your house is bursting at the seams with too many things, then you do not have room for more special ones to come into your life.

Australian comedian, Corrine Grants, tells about being a hoarder and the misery it caused in her book *Lessons in Letting Go: Confessions of a Hoarder*. Ms. Grant said that she hoarded under the mistaken idea that holding onto all of her things would protect her from feelings of guilt and regret. When she got past this, then she was ready to let go and clear up her junk.

A divorced family member of mine could not get past anger and other strong emotions post-divorce and held onto her possessions, accumulating more along the way. It was as if she thought her things were forming a protective cocoon around her. Being in her house was claustrophobic. Sort out emotions along with your unwanted things.

Problem: How to get started clearing one's home and dealing with sentimental items.

Solution: Ms. Grant has this tip: Figure out why you are holding on to too much stuff. Once you figure out what emotions are causing the hoarding, then it is easier to let go. A few friends said getting rid of their children's art and school work, would be like erasing their childhoods. Perhaps these women could keep one spectacular piece from each grade. I saved the special Christmas decorations that my sons made and let go of some of the other stuff. Moving in a hurry made editing these collections much easier.

• Clear away the less painful and insignificant items first. Gain momentum before tackling the bigger, more important stuff. Just keep steadily working on it and do not set up nearly impossible time tables to accomplish this task. I just told myself to clear out and sort one large box every week. Once you have this momentum going, you may surprise yourself and do more. It is like beginning an exercise program, with just walking a short loop first to get started. If one is undecided about some items then box them up and store them for a short period. Not having to make quick decisions about everything can lessen the pressure of downsizing.

• Keep just one article that reminds you of an event, not a trunk full. If you cannot get started, ask a friend or a specialist to help you begin. Your pal does not have the same emotional attachment as you, and can see items in a more objective manner. When you buy something new, that means something has to go out of your house. I have read that many women also apply this to clothes. If getting started is too daunting, then take photos to keep, and later get rid of the actual object.

• Consider having "swap meets" with friends who bring new or gently used clothing or accessories. It is a great way to get rid of items that are not your taste anymore, plus an opportunity to obtain smashing new outfits. Appetizers and wine make it a more festive occasion. Other ones include household goods, which are nice if you lost some in your divorce.

• A way to prevent future clutter is to not bring it into your house. Consider the new trend of renting special outfits for one time occasions like a wedding. Your dress as mother of the bride is memorable and that limits future wearings. There are rental sites online that can mail lovely clothes for a much cheaper price than purchasing it. My friends and I tend to give each other pampering products, since we do not require more knick-knacks. I also give magazine subscriptions to friends. There can be a sense of liberation when you are not bombarded by so much stuff.

25

Post-Divorce Travel Adventures

Vacations with Kids post-Divorce

Vacationing with your kids post-divorce can be done on the cheap if you think "all inclusive." There are no surprises when meals and entertainment are pre-paid and within one's budget. Parents have raved about the Club Meds, which have been around for decades. In some, the youngsters learn various circus skills and put on a show for the guests. The kids happily run around while supervised, and a parent can enjoy reading on the beach. There are other chains of all-inclusive destinations, such as "Beaches Resorts" in the Caribbean. Most include non-motorized sports for free. Dude Ranches is another option for riding and other fun outdoor activities. I have taken my sons to Disneyland on packages that include airfare, hotel, and admission. Sometimes during the slower times of the year, extras are tacked on such as a hundred dollar gift certificate or character breakfast.

Fathers enjoy spending relaxing time with the kids and Royal Caribbean has special "Divorced Dad and Kids" cruises on several of their ships. These are meant to strengthen the bond between father and children. I take my sons on cruises which have a very low price for the 3rd/4th passenger in the same cabin. One is not paying for transportation between cities and the ports of call even please toddlers in strollers. My sons have enjoyed hanging out with new friends from many countries in the kids/teens clubs on board. I go to concerts and lectures and can meet up with my sons at designated times. My divorced mother has also joined us for great family adventures. Holland America is one of the cruise lines that has particularly given us great savings. A savvy travel agent can point you in the right direction or browse various web sites such as Single Parent Travel or Cruisemates.

By Yourself

If you want to get away by yourself, then check out spa packages, such as "Le Divorce" at a resort in the Bahamas which also includes plenty of alcohol with the pampering. "Barefoot Off Shore Sailing School" in the Grenadines has co-ed and all female sailing programs. One divorced woman said there were plenty of others in her all female surfing class at "Surf Diva Camp" in Costa Rica. There is even a camp for women to relive the fun they had as girls in the US.

Consider starting new vacation traditions instead of repeating ones you did pre-divorce. Begin some new memories instead of comparing the past to present. Do not haunt the streets of Paris if that is where you were on your honeymoon. Post-divorced I went on two packaged tours to South Africa and Beijing by myself. I found great companionship and laughter, yet some alone time too.

Forgo expensive dinners for lattes or lunch to increase your Travel Fund. There are various web sites for single travellers if you desire your adventure in a group setting.

Gap Year for Grown-Ups

You may be rattling around in your empty house bemoaning the fact that your youngster has flown the coop. Now can be the opportunity to give your time and make a difference in the world by doing a gap year. Traditionally gap year was done between high school graduation and the first semester of college. Students take up to a year off and embark on a journey around the world. They may volunteer, do a series of short-term jobs or mainly backpack where their whims take them. There are books and web sites that have information on volunteer or gap year for adults. Not only can one have a life changing experience for even two weeks, but can emerge a stronger person. Check and see how long various organizations have been in existence and do a background check to ensure you are selecting the right one. This is also a great chance to see the world for minimal cost. One woman loved her half year in Eastern Europe working in a rural hospital.

Earth Watch has volunteer opportunities around the planet for different skill sets. One couple did scuba diving in Australia counting marine life. Others have worked with veterinarians in Africa taking care of animals. I went to a travel talk on people going to Asia to build houses for just a week or two.

Some newly single aestheticians have travelled the world while working, without incurring transportation costs. They work in the spa on a ship and may have a day off in Singapore or another one in the South Pacific. Steiner of London is one company that trains already experienced aestheticians to work aboard cruise ships. Canyon Ranch has some satellites also on ships. One divorced woman transferred to the international arm of her company and spent time traveling to exotic locales for work. This is the time to try something new, even if for a short time, for valuable self-growth and adventure.

26

Post-Divorce Legal Complications

There are various circumstances why one ex-spouse takes the other one to court. There may be good reasons, such parental alienation or one parent is blocking the other from seeing the kids. There may be an issue of sporadic payments of child support or maintenance. If one has been spreading vicious rumours about the other, they may be hauled into court for slander. Law suits may be out of malice when one has moved on and the other one has not. A well-written and detailed divorce decree can lessen law suits, but cannot guarantee that they will not still occur.

My first court summons was approximately one year after my divorce was finalized. It is shocking for a teenager to answer the door and be asked by the police officer for your phone number or your work address, as what happened to my son. My former spouse represented himself for most of the hearings, so had no legal fees, while mine added up quickly.

If you did not put in your divorce decree that spouses cannot contact the child protective services directly, then there could be a nasty surprise. Our Parenting Plan stipulated that all complaints about the other parent could not be reported directly to any agency, but instead to the court-appointed mediator to sort out and act upon any legitimate ones. This lessened the chance that false allegations would be made about neglect or abuse.

Children's Protective Services are required to check out complaints, no matter how bogus. The problem is that the initial complaint may be lame, but while doing an inspection, other issues might emerge. You can be cited for having too many cats and not enough litter boxes. If a child comes into a parent's room at night to sleep after experiencing nightmares, that can be viewed as pathological. If you are moving and have boxes and piles of stuff everywhere, this constitutes a lack of space and untidy living conditions. Child Protective Services looks at exactly what is (messy house) and not what is happening in the near future (moving next week). These examples are actual cases. It is better to be prepared for what your ex may throw at you and prevent trouble by keeping your house clean and clutter at bay.

You may receive a "Protection from Domestic Abuse," summons which is stating that you committed slander by making disparaging comments which could damage their reputation or social standing in the community. Also, the complaint may contain statements saying that you made false allegations regarding them to the children. The woman in this true story received this particular summons.

It may be tempting to confide parts of your life in order to build a connection with someone else in your similar divorce situation. This can backfire. Pippa is a newly divorced mother who ran into an acquaintance, Ingrid, who was also divorced. Their high school kids were in the same class, and Ingrid's daughter had helped Pippa's son get through his parents' acrimonious divorce. Pippa was quite grateful for this kindness and happily complemented Ingrid regarding her wonderful daughter. Ingrid took the opportunity to go on a rampage about her own ex's shortcomings. Pippa mainly listened and shared just a few of her divorce woes that correlated with what Ingrid had been experiencing. A few months after this conversation, Pippa received a court summons for slander against her ex with Ingrid as his main witness. Ingrid and her family also knew Pippa's ex and someone evidently alerted him about this conversation.

These papers may be accompanied by "Temporary Order of Protection and Order to Appear." One is supposed to cease the perceived offensive behaviour that is named in the summons and appear before a judge. Get an attorney immediately. If you did a collaborative divorce, your attorney may not be able to represent you in this situation, but she can certainly get you to another one. Your attorney may work with your ex's attorney to avoid a court hearing and draft a court document called a "Stipulated Order." Both former spouses agree not to talk about each other and to stay away from each other's residences and job sites. This way it is not one-sided, but the document entered in court is "Petitioner and Respondent" (not vs.) and pertains to both people. If you can avoid going to court, then do so. Court is emotionally draining and costly.

An ex-spouse can file a "Motion for Order to Show Cause" on a specific issue, such as visitation. This type of court summons is filed when a perceived infraction violates what is written in the divorce decree. For example, there may have been child complaints regarding visitation which is now being modified. You are told by an official person, such as the court monitor or therapist, that visitation is being suspended and not to send your child until further notice. The co-parent may file a motion in court accusing you of interfering with visitation. Give your lawyer all the documentation, including emails, so that she can talk to the necessary people, including the therapist and court monitor. She will then file a motion with the court to quash (cancel) the hearing due to supporting documentation, which shows that you did as you were told regarding visitation (i.e., not sending your child).

Post-divorce, it is better to keep personal details private or at least only reveal them to one or two trusted pals. If you cannot be sure who will keep them confidential, then do your unburdening to a professional or to a support group. If your mother or sister are blabbermouths, then share superficial aspects of your life.

27

Self-esteem

"No one can make you feel inferior without your consent."
—Eleanor Roosevelt

People's self-esteem can take a beating in a toxic marriage. One may have been belittled and question their own decisions. A loss of confidence bleeds over into many areas of life. There are ways to boost one's self-esteem and to get back on track. Discover your strengths and follow them to success. Think back into the past to what you used to enjoy doing. One friend had been a painter in her youth, and after her divorce she picked up her paint brush again. Nowadays her paintings grace the walls of several galleries. A few others had a knack for baking and when starting lives over post-divorce, they turned this interest into careers. A career coach can help pinpoint these strengths to get into a fulfilling job.

Post-divorce set new goals and meet these challenges. One divorced friend climbed Mt. Kilimanjaro for a life-changing experience. Others trained and completed marathons. I got a book published. Get out of a comfortable rut and try new endeavours, which in turn increase one's self-worth.

`Sometimes with having a low self-esteem, one can feel that the world is against them. They feel as if they attract trouble, instead of saying, "Well that's life." Reframe a negative outlook into a positive one. Nip negativity in the bud. When I was in an unhappy marriage, I felt like others were judging me and I was coming up short. If someone was abrupt, I assumed that it was something that I had said or done. Post-divorce, I realize that I am not the target of others' rudeness, they are just having an off day. Look for the positives in life and you will encounter them. I see life as a series of fun escapades and adventure now surrounds me post-divorce. Increasing self-esteem is a process that takes time and set goals realistically.

28

Failure is Opportunity in Disguise

"Failure is the opportunity to begin again more intelligently."
—Henry Ford

Some people have said that when they lost their jobs, it seemed like the end of the world. The future looked bleak and they felt like failures. Only later did they realize that this was a gift, feedback that something much better was ready to happen. Oprah Winfrey was fired from her first job as a TV anchor women. Her boss said that she would never make it in TV because she was too emotional. Oprah went on to have a stellar career in that medium.

A few used severance pay to re-train for different jobs, which worked out wonderfully, increasing family time and decreasing stress. Others used the opportunity to retire from the "rat race" and live a simpler lifestyle, choosing to do artistic work or grow an herb garden.

One couple was having difficulty making ends meet selling homemade chocolates in their rural shop. Instead of seeing this as failure, they saw it as feedback, and decided to do something different. They started selling their mouth-watering chocolates online and ultimately did a booming business. They were able to close the shop, which was losing money, and instead do a tremendous trade online. Yes, the few local customers from the shop were still able to buy their chocolates. "When defeat comes accept it as a signal that your plans are not sound, rebuild those plans, and set sail once more toward your coveted goal." Napoleon Hill.

When something is not working out well in life, it may be because you are on the wrong path. Pfizer Pharmaceutical Company had a major failure with a drug trial and feedback indicated that it was not the horrific mistake that it appeared to be. This anti-hypertensive medication's results were so poor that the study was halted early to save money. As per protocol, the study participants were required to return unused medication. Many men refused to do so and then Pfizer discovered the amazing reason why. This former failed drug could not treat hypertension, but worked great for impotence. These blue pills are now called Viagra.

JK Rowling was divorced and nearly destitute when she wrote her Harry Potter novel in an Edinburgh coffee shop. Plenty of publishers turned her down before one decided to take a chance on her book. She persevered when encountering rejection.

Sometimes if one's dream is not materializing despite great effort, one may have to take a different job in order to pay bills. An actor only got sporadic bit parts in Hollywood, so he became a carpenter for many years to support his family. He was making cabinets for a director who gave him a small part in his movie. Then the director hired this carpenter to help read various parts during the auditions for his upcoming film. When Harrison Ford did this, he was hired on the spot to be cast as Han Solo in the *Star Wars* movie. It is frustrating when our goal seems to be just beyond our grasp. Patience is a difficult virtue to obtain. Remember what Helen Keller stated, that when one door closes, another one opens. Life is an adventure, and may include some very rocky roads.

Seeking Employment

"If you hear a voice within you say you cannot paint, then by all means paint, and that voice will be silenced."
— Vincent Van Gogh

Problem: How to jump back into the workforce

Solution: If you lose your job, as I did in my divorce, or if you have been a stay-at-home mom, here are some tips. Is there a business that you frequent regularly? Maybe it's a coffee shop or small retail store. The employers already know and like you and may want you on their work team. It requires a little nerve, but ask if they would consider you for the next job opening. This is what I did and I got hired on the spot. Or they may be able to steer you in another direction, if they are not presently hiring. Once in a while, the fact that you are so nice and seem almost like part of their family can be a drawback. My older son was very close to a couple who owned a local restaurant, where he dined regularly. The couple said that they did not want anything to come in the way of their friendship, so they would not hire him. This may happen to you as well.

• This could be the time to volunteer. If you have empty hours and you offer to volunteer with a charity organization, they will be able to see first-hand what a good worker you are. If a paid position comes up, you are right there to apply for it. Also, some well-connected volunteers may have other job leads.

• Remember other places you patronize, such as the library. Do they have a part-time job available? There are some mothers at a local elementary school who get paid for filling in for the secretary, or doing lunch or playground duty. No, it is not big bucks, but it is something. If you are facing foreclosure or huge divorce fees, jobs you didn't want before will start to look good. Just moving forward with your life will make you feel better and will open up other opportunities.

• Some people try temp work, which can lead to a permanent position. This could be the time to do an internship to learn new job skills, thus increasing your marketability. If you do an internship in your field, the staff can give you job leads, if they are not hiring presently. A friend's daughter was unable to get a job in her field after her graduation from college. She accepted an unpaid internship and the company liked her so well that she was offered a job right after it ended. You may want to do an internship or apprenticeship in a totally new area, such as with a florist, to see if a change in careers would be the ticket.

• Look in the classified ad section of your newspaper. Perhaps you did not think of a type of job in your area of interest or hobby. Are you great at crafts? Check for a job opening at a bead or knitting shop, if that is your talent. Find a clothing store, if you have a flair for fashion, even if you have never pursued that area before. Think positively, and be creative and flexible. You will find something.

• Most likely you will need to spruce up your résumé (CV). Volunteering can be valuable on a résumé, especially if you utilized skills from your degree or work history. My community college has a free résumé service and did an excellent job with mine, including printing it on parchment paper. Some teachers provide this service for a reasonable price. The adviser there had some job ideas and helped me write two great cover letters. Remember to always include a cover letter, specific to that job. When I ran a business, I tossed any job applications that did not include one.

• Your community college may provide vocational aptitude testing to determine your strengths and best possible careers. They can give occupational advice or steer you in the right direction. It is important to do a realistic assessment of your job skills to see which areas could improve. You may need to brush up on computer skills. Are you proficient with professional social media sites, such as LinkedIn?

• Enlist a savvy friend or a personal shopper to spruce up your work wardrobe. Select a few special outfits to wear to job interviews. When I co-owned a business, I called a mature woman with loads of work experience who had completed an application, for an interview. She arrived in stretch pants and a wrinkled blouse. Needless to say, I did not hire her. Consider doing a mock interview as practice, if you have been out of the work world for a while. One woman told me that she did an online search for the ten most popular interview questions. All were asked in her interview and she got that dream job.

Watch the hilarious movie, "Nine to Five" about madcap antics in the workplace. Dolly Parton and Lily Tomlin are joined by Jane Fonda's recently divorced character, who is at a new job, after a long work hiatus.

29

Ways to Lower Stress and Boost Well-Being

"We hide part of ourselves, when we lie about how we feel. The normal stress associated with lying is compounded by the stress of suppressing emotions." *Australia's Women's Weekly* Magazine (December, 2009). One can reply "I'm surviving" and leave at that when questioned on how well one is doing.

Set aside ten to twenty minutes a day that you will worry. Banish thoughts of worry to this daily time period. Write down your thoughts before you go to sleep and note any actions that you will do the following day.

Be in nature, take a hike, or eat your lunch in the park. Studies have indicated being in the green outdoors reduces anger, aggression and stress. Blood pressure and stress hormones decrease in this bucolic setting. A study out of the University of Essex discovered that 88% of subjects had an increased improvement in their mood with only five minutes of walking outside in nature as opposed to in the mall. The researchers recommend "green therapy" daily to improve mental and physical health and lower the stress hormone, cortisol. Stroll around a park or have a picnic in a leafy area.

When you need help, ask for it. Trying to do everything around the house, your children's school, or work can be an unrealistic goal and can also be a detriment to your health. Just say no or explain what you realistically can do.

Taking on too much, whether running the concession stand at school, or being president of your professional organization, can be overwhelming during divorce. Volunteer for an hour timeslot or offer to do a small task.

Do yoga to clear the mind and strengthen the body. Eat dark chocolate (containing antioxidants) and food with magnesium. Pamper yourself with massages, facials and pedicures.

If you have the means and opportunity, get away to a special place to help you relax and be fully present in the moment. Go to a spa with girlfriends. Have your heart rate increased by a roller coaster ride, rather than by the anxiety of worrying about what is just around the corner with your divorce. Anticipating where I will go on my next holiday immediately boosts my well-being.

Buy a relaxation CD, which guides you on how to relax, so you do not have to think about it. I like the ones which start at the feet and move up the body to the head. These CDs have you tense a body part and then totally relax it. You may even fall asleep during this. Other CDs have soothing sounds, like whales or rain. Take some deep breaths to release tension and focus on the sounds.

Meditation

Meditation enables you to be more serene in stressful divorce situations and to analyse information in a calmer manner. Meditation can be done in different ways and you may opt to try various methods. A Buddhist monk, Olanda Ananda, who holds seminars globally, has these suggestions. He emphasized concentrating on your breath. Next, realize that you will have thoughts. He said to deal with these thoughts as if they were passing clouds, and just let them drift by. Clear your mind, concentrate on the individual breaths and do not let any thoughts linger. The more you meditate, the easier it becomes to keep your mind serene.

Other forms of meditation include repeating a mantra (a saying or word) or chanting. If you are in an ashram in India, you may be chanting in their language. The purpose of meditation is to still your mind, which helps you to deal with life's situations more calmly. Your blood pressure and heart rate can even decrease with regular practice of these techniques.

Be immersed in the moment and quiet the inner chatter. When entering Disneyland, there is a sign saying that you are leaving today and entering yesterday, tomorrow and fantasy. What a great reminder to be in the moment, have fun, plus leave your stress and worries of today behind. Be like your children or younger self and be fully immersed in the situation.

Visualization

Visualization has you relax mentally and go to an inviting place, such as the beach or an Alpine meadow. Sit in a comfortable chair and close your eyes. Take several deep breaths. Inhale tranquillity and exhale tension. See tranquillity as a colour, such as a blue. Exhale tension as a colour, such as a dark grey or black. Relax your body, continuing to take deep cleansing breathes, inhaling tranquillity blue and exhaling tension dark grey.

For example, mentally walk along the beach and feel the warm, grainy sand under your feet and between your toes. Take a deep breath and inhale the salty air. Feel a gentle breeze ruffle your hair and the warm sunshine on your upturned face. Notice the incredible spectrum of blues and greens of the water. See the foamy waves hitting the shoreline. Hear the roar of the waves and the cries of the sea gulls. Feel moved by the beauty of the scene and the serenity it brings you. You are relaxed. Taste the occasional spray of salt water as it hits your tongue. Involve all of your senses in visualization.

You can go back to this place mentally whenever you want a refuge of calmness and relaxation. Later, when you are entering a courtroom or an attorney's office, go back to your special place. Be there and feel the calmness, bringing this feeling with you into different situations.

Imagine yourself out of pain. Here is a tip from the Neuro-Linguistic Programming (NLP) world to get rid of pain. Think of pain as a colour. Maybe your intense headache is a black colour. Now give it a shape. For example, you might imagine your headache as black smoke. Next, pick an area of your body that is comfortable and give that feeling a colour. Then imagine it as a shape. For instance, the comfortable feeling may be a blue sphere.

Imagine the black smoke of headache pain leaving the top of your head, like black smoke billowing out of a chimney. In its place, move the comfortable blue sphere up through your body, filling up your head with a pleasant sensation. Take some deep breathes, breathing out whatever does not feel good (black smoky headache pain) and breathing in tranquillity. Think of a favourite vacation place and do the above visualization exercise. This visualization also works well with kids and helps distract them if they are at the dentist or in other unpleasant situations.

Songs in Divorce

Throughout history people have marched into war with music and songs. As early as 1396, the Scottish clans used a form of bagpipes in battles, which was heard at least several miles away. In the American Revolution, songs helped the people to rally around the cause. Songs can soothe you or be your battle cry during your divorce. They can represent how you are feeling. One woman stated that tribal music with a distinctive beat gets her moving and ready to face any adversity.

During my difficult divorce, when I heard Tom Petty's, "I won't back down...I'll stand my ground," it motivated me to hang in there and spend the extra time digging through records to prove my points. I felt like I could handle what was thrown at me and "stand my ground." Also, the Tom Petty song, "Don't Come around Here No More," fits the bill about not wanting to see my ex. My boys said to add, "I Will Survive" (Gloria Gaynor), to my list and yes, I was surviving and that became my mantra. Post-divorce, The Who's "I'm Free" is such an empowering song. Any Aretha Franklin ditty will do, especially "Respect." Pick some songs that represent you and your situation. Post-divorce my mantra is Cyndi Lauper's "Girls Just Want to have Fun." A great song for any situation, which can turn your stressful day around is "What a Wonderful World" by Louis Armstrong. It is upbeat with such a powerful, joyful message.

Laugh your Way to Better Health

"A little nonsense now and then is relished by the wisest men."
—Roald Dahl

At Cancer Treatment Centres of America, CTCA, "Laughter Therapy" is an integral part of the cancer treatment. Having fun and laughing boost the immune system, increasing natural killer cells, which destroy tumour cells. Laughter aids in increasing one's positive outlook on life, which is important particularly when facing challenges like cancer or divorce. Having fun connects you to others and various studies have indicated the positive affect of socialization on longevity.

Laughter reduces stress and raises one's immunity. A higher immunity helps to fight off viruses more efficiently. The New England Journal of Medicine states that laughter reduces the bad cholesterol (LDH) and raises the good cholesterol (HDL). It also reduces blood pressure, and the stress hormone cortisol. Laughter increases the release of endorphins, which are neurotransmitters that help us feel good, like opiates that reduce pain. Muscles become relaxed, more oxygen and blood circulate around one's body which increases blood flow to the heart. This leads to improving the quality of sleep. One acquaintance had TMJ pain and when she had a fit of laughter, the pain completely went away. So go out and enjoy that comedy, because you are boosting your health.

Norman Cousins wrote the book, *Anatomy of an Illness*. He had been incapacitated by a spinal column illness and was in great pain. He tried both conventional and holistic types of remedies without a cure. For one month he closeted himself away and watched comedies and read jokes. After that time period, he presented himself to his stunned doctors who could not find a trace of the disease.

Oxford University did a study where participants either watched a comedy or a documentary. After these shows, the researchers applied either very cold or painful pressure to the subjects' arms. The people who watched the comedies and laughed hard, withstood 10% more pain or cold than the other subjects who did not experience the belly laughs.

When I was in the throes of divorce, I borrowed the movie *The First Wives Club* and laughed all the way through it. This film should be a requirement for women going through divorce. I was almost fifty and the actresses, Bette Midler, Diane Keaton and Goldie Hawn, all turned fifty while filming this movie. Besides being hilarious, the message was not revenge, but justice. My two sons heard my laughter, and when I was finished, asked if they could view it also. I put this movie right back in and chuckled through it again, along with my sons. *The First Wives' Club* changed my outlook on my divorce process, turning it partly into an absurd comedy. My spouse was mentally cast into the role of a cartoon character.

A great book, also humorous, and with the same message, is Elizabeth Buchan's, *Revenge of the Middle Age Woman*. I had read it previously, but enjoyed it immensely the second time around during my divorce. The character lives in London and loses her husband and job, as I did. She gets her revenge by turning her life around. This novel is a must read.

Connection between Language and Well-Being

I worked in a busy trauma unit and kept saying that I needed a break. Well, I got a nice, long six week break with a broken foot. My subconscious heard that I wanted a break and literally followed that directive. Your subconscious mind is looking for your word choice to give it direction. Just admit to anger or frustration and leave it at that. You have heard, "Be careful what you wish for, because you may get it." Well I sure did.

Notice the link between words to the body part that hurts. Do not connect your angry words with a specific body location. One woman complained about various people who were a "pain in the neck." She has chronic neck pain.

My teenage son would say, "He really pisses me off," and then developed a problem "pissing" in a public bathroom (medically known as "shy bladder"). After I pointed out the connection between his use of words and his "pissing" problem, the shy bladder became a thing of the past.

One older, very healthy family friend kept saying he/she's a "corker" when someone was a bit maddening or out of control. So instead of declaring negatively, "He'll give me a stroke someday," say positively, "He's a corker."

Word choice is important on an emotional level. Avoid using "afraid" or "fear" in a casual way. Do not say, "I am afraid that my alimony check will be late again" or "I fear my boss will be in a bad mood today." If the boss is in a bad mood, that is his problem, but not your fear. Do not state "I live in fear that…" and usually it is about something trivial. Demonstrate being empowered by your vocabulary.

Another aspect of language is to have it point you towards a goal, not what you do not want to do. If your goal is to remember to take your book back to the library, then say, "I must remember my book," Not "I can't forget my book." You do not want the two words "forget" and "book" together in your subconscious mind. An example of this concept is when Lindsey's husband was going to Beijing for a business trip and she wanted him to bring her back a t-shirt. Instead of saying what designs she wanted (her goal), she told him what she did not like. Lindsey said,

"Bring me back a t-shirt with any scene on it except the Great Wall of China." When Drew got to Beijing, he remembered that Lindsey wanted a t-shirt and had said something about The Great Wall of China. Yes, that is the t-shirt Lindsey received.

Positive words lead to the desired outcome and, with a little practice, this becomes easier. Avoid making statements about what you do not wish to happen. Instead put your energy into thoughts like "I will get the xyz investment with my divorce." Have your language point you in the direction of your goal.

A school district spent about $40,000 writing a conduct code manual which included bullying behaviour and its consequences. This took months to complete. When the committee went over the final results, the whole project had to be scrapped and redone. The entire manual contained "don't" statements with behaviours that were unacceptable, not clear instructions about what was expected.

Using positive language of what is expected is a more effective way to deal with children. "Bums in the chair" or feet on the floor" is clearer than stating what you do not want, "don't run around." I received a call from my son saying, "Where are you?" I had said that I could NOT pick him up, and later he remembered something about picking him up. Stating "walk home from school today" (desired outcome) would have been the way to go. Use upbeat language to help you envision your dreams.

Stop using the "S" word, "should." Many times the word "should" is a relic from our childhood. It may be parents saying that we "should" do this and that and we feel guilty as adults. You have enough on your plate going through divorce proceedings without worrying about doing even more. Should can imply trying to please others and putting your wants and needs on the back burner. Saying you "should" do an action may indicate that you feel judged by others. One has choices and is not obligated to live up to others' standards. Drop "should" from your vocabulary and use other words like, "No, I am overloaded right now" or "Yes, I am able to make homemade lasagne today."

30 Health Issues with Divorce

Cardiac Issues, Panic Attacks and Stroke

Stress can cause or exacerbate heart arrhythmias, such as atrial fibrillation. You may notice a fluttering in your chest or an occasional skipping of a beat in your heart. If these are rare, isolated incidents then get more rest, hydration and nutrition. If a progression or frequency of symptoms (such as dizziness), starts to occur, then contact your doctor. Medication could be needed if these episodes increase. An EKG may be ordered or an ultrasound performed to rule out any serious problems. Starting a program to reduce stress is beneficial.

The question sometimes arises in divorce as to the difference between a panic attack and a heart attack. The classic sign of a heart attack in women vs. men is back pain. So many females have said, "I did not have chest or jaw pain, and no pain radiated down my left arm." If you suddenly start having back pain, often accompanied with nausea, get to a hospital. One retired nurse, who later died from a massive MI, waited six hours before calling her daughter while suffering from intense lower back pain and vomiting. The cardiologist said that if she had gotten to the hospital at the onset of these symptoms, her prognosis would have been fairly good.

If a young woman has a history of panic attacks, then that is probably what is happening. A panic attack comes on suddenly, with a feeling of anxiety, breathlessness and mild chest discomfort. Some women have described these being accompanied by a feeling of doom. It is better to go to the hospital with a panic attack, then to err and not go to the ER when it is really a heart attack. I had a stressed out young woman squirt Bach's Rescue Remedy into her mouth during an intense panic attack. This calmed her down enough to walk out to her friend's car for a ride to urgent care.

If you suddenly cannot think of common words and have numbness or drooping on one side, this could be the onset of a stroke. Think "star" and have the person do the following to determine the possibility of a stroke:

S smile, to see if it is lopsided.

T tongue, stick out the tongue, to see if it goes to one side.

A arms, hold arms straight out in front, to see if one drops.

R repeat simple phrases.

Get to the ER immediately if any of these are abnormal.

The Importance of Sleep in Divorce

Both Delta (Slow Wave Sleep) and particularly REM (Rapid Eye Movements) stages of sleep assist with processing and storing new memories and learning. During sleep the neural connections that form memories are strengthened. REM sleep is associated with the brain's cerebral cortex, which is responsible for learning and organizing information. REM sleep is like a secretary who organizes and purges files, delegating less important ones to the archives. Various studies have indicated when REM sleep is deficient, then newly learned skills may be forgotten.

New research indicates that REM increases activity in the brain's right hemisphere, which is linked to creativity. Scientist James Watson co-discovered the double helix shape of DNA after a dream of two snakes intertwined. Others, such as Thomas Edison, had bursts of creativity in dreams that contributed to inventions.

In deep sleep, the growth hormone is released. Delta sleep increases the production of proteins which are essential for cell growth and the ability to repair any cellar damage. New studies are indicating the link between less deep sleep to weight gain and the condition of pre-diabetes. Lack of sleep has a negative effect on the immune system. Adequate Delta sleep enhances bodily functions, repair, and rejuvenation.

Sleep deprivation can lead to irritability and cognitive problems, where new information is less remembered. Decisions and social interactions can be impaired. The divorce process requires important decisions with lifelong repercussions to be made as calmly as possible. Several executives have written about scheduling seven to eight hours of sleep time into their agenda to ensure peak performance.

Dealing with Insomnia

You particularly require regular sleep during your divorce, so here are a few tips on beating insomnia, which can result from a myriad of causes.

Talk to a therapist or get out more with friends to share confidences and laughter. Try Yoga, meditation or Tai Chi. Every morning, I do Qi Gong stretches and breathing, which activate energy points. Since practicing it, my back issue is a thing of the past. In 1989, China recognized Qi Gong as a standard of medical treatment and it is currently offered on their National Health Plan. It greatly reduces stress.

Sleep apnoea is when breathing stops for a few moments and your brain wakes you up to start breathing again. The muscles in the back of the throat relax and occlude the airway. Sleeping on one's side or in more severe cases, wearing a CPAP mask, can alleviate this condition. Other medical reasons for insomnia include chronic pain or having to get up at night to go to the toilet. Work with your doctor on these issues and limit your liquid intake before bedtime.

Insomnia can be started by worrying, which becomes a habit and a vicious cycle. Break this cycle by having a regular bedtime, with planned winding down and relaxing beforehand. Ditch watching the news before bedtime. The news will still be there in morning. Sleep in a dark, quiet and cool temperature bedroom, with your clock out of your view. When I have a difficult time getting to sleep or if I wake up in the middle of the night, Bach's Sleep Rescue Remedy helps me. Some people write down their worries or the next day's to do list, which allows them to stop worrying and then have uninterrupted sleep.

I was having difficulty sleeping through the night and was waking up after every REM (dream) cycle. I longed to feel well rested in the mornings. When I adjusted my bedtime to my night owl circadian rhythm, this problem was eliminated. I usually go to bed at midnight or later and have a lot more energy now. Tweaking your bedtime to your natural sleep/wake cycle can lessen insomnia.

One celebrity was asked if his worries kept him up at night. He said that he worried only in the daytime. When it was his bedtime he told God, "Hey, since you're going to be up all night, take over my worries and I'll get them back in the morning." I tried his solution and it works for me.

Psychological issues, such as depression or bipolar disorder, can cause insomnia, as can the medications that treat them. Contact your doctor to adjust your dose or switch to a similar, but different medication. Regular exercise, such as walking, boosts your mood and your endorphins.

31

Grief and Loss Post-Divorce

Grief

Grief seems to especially hit a few months to a year after the divorce is finalized and can take people by surprise. Even after leaving an abusive marriage, people have still gone through the stages of grief. Recognize that you will have grief in some degree, no matter how you feel about your ex. Grief is a sense of loss, whether it is for a person, or a former way of life. Dr. Elisabeth Kubler-Ross explains the grief process in her excellent book, *On Death and Dying*. The stages are "anger, denial, bargaining, depression" (some therapists say the latter is anger turned inwards) and "acceptance." The emotions run into each other and one can shift back and forth between the stages. These stages are pertinent to divorce, or having a major upheaval.

A loss or change in relationships post-divorce is one more part of grief. Understand that this will happen in varying degrees. Grief does lessen with time, whether it is with divorce or death. Boiron has homeopathic medicine for grief which helped me when my mother and cats died. Bach's Flower Remedies also include remedies that can help make grief more manageable. Discuss your situation with a naturopath to get the best one for you.

One British woman wrote about her charmed life in a beautiful country village. She loved volunteering, being in the community and spending time with her neighbours. When her husband suddenly left her, she went through the stages of grief until she eventually reached the stage of acceptance and hope. This Brit learned to accept and deal with the reality of her situation. She moved to London, got a job, met new neighbours and started looking forward to planning things for the future. She found joy in life and put the painful past behind her.

A person can get stuck in one stage, benefiting from a therapist, a life coach or a support group. Ways of dealing with grief:

Exercise, eat nutritious food and get plenty of rest.

Help yourself emotionally by getting outside to a park or going hiking.

Get a massage, facial or pedicure.

Vent your anger/sadness.

Realize that holidays can have unrealistic expectations—entertaining, spending increased time with family, putting on a cheerful holiday face when that is not how you really feel. You may be grieving for your old way of life, and this may be more painful during the holiday season. Express your needs and feelings to others and ask for their support.

Ex-spouses and Past Loves

Dopamine, a neurotransmitter which helps regulate emotion, is increased when one falls in love, does something enjoyable or has a new adventure. So, if your ex is still living in your head rent-free, do something new to increase your dopamine level. Take a fun class, such as Zumba, up your exercise time or go to an exotic destination. Looking at your ex's photos, checking their Facebook page or reading old love letters will not help you to move on. Get rid of, or at least gather up photos and mementos and store them out-of-sight, such as at your parents' house to deal with at a later time. Naomi had a few nice family photos with her ex in them. She skilfully edited her ex right out of them and can enjoy these pictures now. My mother, husband, sons and I had a few lovely professional portraits taken on some cruises. After removing my ex from these photographs, I discovered it was as if he had never embarked on these voyages with us. Our vacation memories deleted him out of these journeys and we laugh at these good times.

One may long to escape the turmoil of divorce and relive a more pleasant time. This leads to fantasizing about the one who got away. He may have been a high school crush or she could be the one you let go of in college. Comprehending what the one who got away represents, will give insight to what is now lacking in your life. It may not be the person himself that you are mourning, but rather your younger carefree self who was not overwhelmed with life's burdens. Does that relationship conjure up feelings of fun and light-heartedness that is missing nowadays? Thinking hard about the reason you two parted can give a reality check regarding why you did not get married. Our memories tend to gloss over the bad bits, resulting in seeing past relationships with rose coloured glasses.

Identity Changes with Divorce

Loss is part of divorce, and this can include one's identity. If you own a business together, you may go from co-owner to unemployed, especially if your spouse is the lawyer or doctor, and you were the support staff. One has to find a new job. The trick is reinventing yourself, and discovering hidden talents for your metamorphosis.

One young man married the boss's daughter after he had been at the business for several years. He enjoyed his job and loved the buzz of being in Hollywood. His wife started having affairs soon after being married and they ended up divorced. This fellow in his late twenties, was fired from his job during his divorce. His identity changed to unemployed and he finds it depressing not being able to find a job in his same line of work.

Mary enjoyed the perks that went along with being a doctor's wife, such as the role of stay-at-home mother. She was in a horrendous car accident which left her needing physical therapy for months. Her husband started an affair with his secretary and filed for divorce while Mary was still recovering. She lost her connection to the social life of the medical community and volunteer position at the hospital (too painful to run into ex). Mary's identity of stay-at-home mother changed to part-time employee, when she found a job post-divorce. I have heard similar stories along this line, with women married to various other professionals.

Some women from long-term marriages regretted losing their housewife identity post-divorce. This involved missing a sense of structure in their lives, and feeling adrift without the comfort of their usual routine. It takes time learning to enjoy the freedom of not catering to a partner's needs.

I have a long-time acquaintance that is back in my life after a hiatus. I asked her what had happened, since we regularly got together at a mutual friend's house. She said "Did you ever see me at LeAnn's after my divorce?" Well, no actually. She asked when the last time that I had been to LeAnn's house. Oh, it was before my divorce too. Although

LeAnn and I get together with our "coffee club," I had never been invited back to her house for events, as married friends had been.

It is probably subconscious, but LeAnn entertains as if on Noah's Ark, everyone is in pairs. You may bump up against this type of situation, where you are dropped from a couple's invitation list. Do not take it personally and see if you can meet your friend for a latte instead.

One woman was known around her small community as "John's wife." She started her own business and was building a good reputation when she got divorced. Phyllis opted to keep her husband's last name post-divorce since that was tied to her business recognition. In another case, a lawyer friend opted to keep her husband's last name when divorced, since that was the name of her law firm. Others gave a variation of "I wanted to be identified as the same clan as my children," so kept the same surname. Many others could not wait to go back to their maiden names. Identity is a personal matter, so use what name works best for you. If you are going back to your maiden surname, be sure to put this name change in the divorce decree. Otherwise, you have the expense and hassle of going to court post-divorce to get this accomplished.

One's former identity is gone, so allow yourself to mourn this loss. Express your feelings to your support system or to a life coach. Examine other roles in your life, such as colleague, daughter and volunteer, to expand them. Recognize and acknowledge the roles that you do well, such as coolest aunt on the planet or events coordinator at your office. When you lose an identity, seek out new ones by volunteering or becoming a member of a new group. I joined MeetUp.com. Some divorced friends joined book clubs. Discover what is blocking you from leaving the past behind and exploring new opportunities and friendships.

Seek out people and activities that support your single status.

32

Changes in Relationships with Divorce

<u>Losing Some Friends and Becoming Closer to Others</u>

Some friendships may change after your divorce. If there were some abuse in your marriage and you shared that with friends, it is dismaying to discover they still want to maintain relationships with each of you. This happened to me and my friend still said "I love both of you", when she rarely had seen my husband. Had to decline invitations to her house post-divorce because she also included my ex. Divorce tends to separate your true friends from others.

Friends may distance themselves from you because they do not want to become involved or are scarce for other reasons. Lara had a friend that she met for lunch over the years. When Lara started her divorce proceedings and shared some abuse that her husband committed, this friend kept saying, "I can't believe it." Lara was quite surprised when her phone calls were not returned and a tentatively planned lunch never happened. A few months later, Lara's husband told their daughters that he and this friend were a couple. They got married after the divorce was finalized.

Reevaluate your friendships to see if they have run their course or are truly beneficial. I had a friend who continued to talk a lot about her ex years later. When I was going through a divorce, she became fixated on mine, calling almost daily for updates. When she abruptly disappeared for months and then reappeared I asked her why. She said that I had snapped at her on the phone a few days before I was moving and nobody had done that to her before. I am sure that I snapped at anyone in my path because moving and divorce proceedings are a toxic combination. My other friends gave me some slack with my rising stress level and were supportive. That friendship soon fizzled.

Mourn the loss of friendships, but determine if it is the person or the activities that you did with them, that you really miss. Sometimes friendships that are based on a particular interest or aspect of your life, are no longer relevant post-divorce. How does one disentangle herself from a friend? There are several ways – indirect and direct. If a friend who is constantly in crisis mode – refuses to listen to yours, or be supportive, then cut the tie. You can stop taking her calls or e-mails. Perhaps be direct and tell her that you are not available, due to dealing with your own circumstance. Friendship is about give and take – do not mainly be on the giving end, especially when going through a tough transition.

What if a friendship is limping along? This can be handled by spacing get-togethers months apart until they eventually cease. If she asks why this is happening, state you are in a busy time and have to take a break to concentrate on your situation. Be aware that you may be the one dropped because you are not going to parties or on endless shopping sprees post-divorce. This hurts, but it makes space in your life for more meaningful relationships to enter.

If you are hanging onto too many people, whom you only see out of habit, you may not have room for more meaningful relationships to enter your life. Limit your time with energy vampires who drain you, and spend it with positive people instead.

Changes in Family Dynamics

You may find that divorce similarly prunes your family tree. Some relatives may harbour anger towards you, and your divorce is just another thing to hold against you. Their unkindness and lack of support is their issue, although it can be difficult for you. Your divorce may trigger painful memories of theirs and they might avoid you so as not to relive them. If you have unsupportive relatives that are difficult to avoid, limit your visits to one hour every month or so. Consider meeting in a public place where they are more apt to be better behaved. You then have the option of leaving quickly if they become rude. One could limit contact to just holiday cards, if seeing them is truly dreadful, or if they are clearly in your ex's camp.

Clarice's step-sister, Babs, resented her since they were children. Clarice escaped from an abusive marriage and was quite vulnerable post-divorce. Babs cut Clarice out of her life stating that "there were two sides to the story." This step-sister upped her social media contact with that ex. In another case, Jennifer's stepmother was directly informed of her grandsons' abuse including molestation. The boys told this woman that it was hurtful if she decided to stay in touch with their abusive father and that they would not be able to share much of their lives with her. When the step-grandmother mentioned that their father felt hurt, they pulled away and sent cards. The step-grandmother continued to criticize the grandsons' choice of not having a relationship with their father, so Jennifer terminated ties with this unsupportive woman. There can be tough decisions to make regarding family post-divorce. Accept that you cannot change people, including relatives. Giving explanations of what transpired, including abuse, is fine.

The way they choose to react to this information is their right, however hurtful it may be to you.

Naomi's Aunt Mae does not have children and lives across the country from her. During visits, Naomi would spend a lot of time with Aunt Mae, who definitely prefers male to female company. After the divorce, this aunt came to town and stayed in a hotel, choosing to spend time with Naomi's ex and his family. She said that they entertained her so much that she was too tired to get together with Naomi and her children. Now this aunt does not even send cards.

One woman was close to her nieces by marriage, and was devastated when her husband left her for another woman. These nieces declared that Dana was to "get custody" of them in the divorce and continue to have a warm relationship with her today.

As time goes by, some former couples do occasionally get together with new spouses and children, sometimes at a former in-law's house. Some parents remain friends and good co-parents, so seeing family and mutual friends is not an issue.

Banish Childhood Patterns with Family

Sometimes dialogue within our family runs like an old script. Instead of reacting to the words, clarify their meaning or motivation. If your mother has the same script about eating a certain way, consider what is behind it. Say something along the line of "I know you have my best interests at heart, but my doctor approves of my being a vegetarian and my cholesterol level is excellent. I eat very healthy and balanced meals. Thank you for your concern, and now we don't have to discuss this subject again, since we have clarified that I am very healthy and fit." If your brother is usually harping on you spending too freely, address his concern and say "I contribute monthly to my savings and retirement accounts. I have a great financial advisor, so we do not have to talk about my financial situation again. Thanks for your concern." If your aunt is nosey, say "I am not sure why you would need to know that information, but I am doing fine." Do not participate when family members use the same script to bring up criticisms again and again. You be the catalyst for change and feel free to shorten family visits.

Accept your parents and move on with your life. After divorce, one is starting life anew and this is the time to break old childhood patterns of interactions with family members. Many of us seek in new relationships what we did not receive from our parents. Realize that parents have their shortcomings and may not have given us the foundation in life that we felt we deserved. Some people have built a close-knit network of companions who function as if an extension of their family. Whatever love and support that was not given by parents, is now bestowed by this circle of friends. If there is a gap in your life regarding family, then plug it up with friends.

You can change your reactions and behaviour, not someone else's. Refuse to participate in old childhood patterns. If the same arguments erupt, remove yourself by taking a walk, or change your response. Try being nonchalant like, "Yeah, perhaps I do," and change the subject. Act bored or laid back, so the family sees that they cannot get a rise out of you. Make a joke or bring humour to the situation. Distraction can steer the communication in a better direction. Have a few current news topics or juicy bits of trivia to toss out when you are the target of criticism.

If things are truly awful, then leave.

33

Facing Life's Transitions Post-Divorce

<u>Empty Nest</u>

Facing an Empty Nest after losing a spouse through divorce can be overwhelming. Expect to mourn for the loss of what was and may never be again. This is one monumental change to deal with without the support of a close adult right in your house. Married friends have a person (spouse) right on the spot to do spontaneous activities with, such as going to a film or out to lunch when melancholy hits. I have sympathetic cats who like to snuggle, but not go out for lattes. Divorce and widowed people said it is a quiet house that sparks loneliness. A little solitude is fine, but it goes on and on.

Problem: Feeling lonely in a quiet house when your last child has just left.

Solution: Schedule something fun for immediately after your child leaves. I had a pampering facial prescheduled hours after mine left for college. The next morning a friend met me for lattes and another one for a movie later. It is easier if one has fun events to anticipate for at least the first few days.

• Start a group up of other Empty Nesters for fun and mutual support. Penny, a stay-at-home mother, was bereft when her youngest went off to college. This happened when her oldest son was getting married and contemplating a move to another city. Penny called the mothers of her son's classmates and formed a group that meets once a month. At first it was for tears, but now it is for laughter and companionship. These women claim that getting together is much cheaper than therapy.

• Distraction is the key to beating loneliness with the Empty Nest Syndrome. Starting new activities is paramount to thriving in this transition. Start a class, whether it is for a special interest or possible career change or advancement. Some mothers have taken cooking or cake decoration classes which were fun and led to making some extra cash selling delicious goodies to time-strapped peers. I took computer classes to brush up on using social media and Power point. A woman went back to school to change careers when her youngest was almost ready to fly the nest. She was so engrossed in her classwork and later on, student teaching, that she barely had time to think about her two kids in college. This is the time to reinvent yourself and rediscover long lost passions.

• Wait and tackle big projects after your kid goes off to school, such as organizing and cleaning out your basement or garage. I bought bins and shelves and went to town. It is so much easier to find gardening supplies, holiday lights, plus much more. A friend who is an avid gardener, waited to do a big landscaping project as her daughter was leaving. Whether you remained in your house post-divorce or are in a new one, if you have considered redecorating, this may be a good moment.

- Have a foreign exchange student live with you for a few months or for a school year. You then have a young person around who requires maternal advice and care. You will learn about their culture and may end up with another family member for life. One co-worker said, after all of the laundry she did and meals she made, this exchange kid will be in her life forever. She has made several trips to Rome for visiting and events. She claims that she now has an extended family in Italy. What a fabulous way to avoid the Empty Nest Syndrome.

- Expand your social or professional networks. I joined two MeetUp.com groups and get together nearly every week. The conversations are stimulating with these intelligent folks. I am a new member of Toastmasters International, to help prepare me for my radio interviews and speaking engagements. It also helps my self-esteem and my communication skills.

- Start some new programs, such as a fitness regime. The boost in endorphins will be an added benefit to a fitter body. I began Zumba and do Tai Chi as an Empty Nester. Take a trip with friends who also may be new Empty Nesters. Consider visiting your old college roommate or other pals from the past.

-

Family Member's Death or Illness Post-Divorce

One can still be reeling after a divorce, yet have to deal with a family member knocking on death's door. It is hard to be grounded and centred enough to make end-of-life decisions for someone else when one's life seems to be topsy-turvy. Look at what you can do realistically, and do not let guilt or others drive you to take on more than you can. If you have a breakdown, then you are no use to the ill family member.

My mother had a heart attack a year after my divorce. She had been in denial about the whole thing, and did not want to hear about what my sons and I had gone through both pre and post-divorce. One of my sons just revealed more abuse, and my mother could no longer justify her neutral behaviour. She could not sit on the fence, but had to come to her grandson's aid and be a pillar of support. The night she was transferred to the CCU from the ER, her ex son-in-law came into her room. After his visit, she phoned me for help and we put him on a "no visitor" list, but she was already quite agitated by then and had a full cardiac code the next day. A bit later, she was discharged to a convalescent home, because there was no way that I could take care of her for most of the day. I had an acute situation with my son and was already at the breaking point. Do what you can and ignore unhelpful advice and judgments.

My mother came home for about two weeks, and I cooked some and saw her every day. Then she had a stroke and went back to the hospital, then convalescent home and was placed in Hospice. If you are in a similar situation, I highly recommend Hospice as much for your support as for your loved ones. You can speak to non-judgmental professionals who will help you sort out the whole situation plus available financial services. Not once did they question any of my decisions. A few people criticized me for not becoming her full-time care-giver.

Several women I know lost twin sisters post-divorce, and this was quite a blow. When they required extra nurturing, they gave it instead. When facing imminent death of loved ones or long-term care, consider speaking to a professional. Hospitals have counsellors and chaplains on board who deal with this every day and can be your anchor in turbulent seas. Several others claim having their mothers in high quality long-term care facilities has been the best choice in their situations. My mother enjoyed having musical programs and parties that we could attend with her. Do what you feel is best.

Problem: Feeling overwhelmed post-divorce, when a loved one is gone.

Solution: After a death, be kind to yourself. Do not dwell in guilt that you did not do enough. You did a tremendous job under stress with the skills that you possessed. Yes, there were actions I could have done differently, but in the long run the outcome still would have been the same. Before my mother passed, my sons told her to leave dimes for us. Now finding dimes in weird places lets my sons know that she is watching over them. It brings them comfort and laughter. Some people have found other objects that they feel were sent by their deceased person. If this is not in your belief system that is fine.

Do what brings you closure and comfort, such a walk in a beautiful park or enjoying luscious chocolate. My sons and I travelled to several places that had been on my mother's top ten list. We told funny stories about her in London as we walked around Green Park. We were still laughing in Richoux Piccadilly, her favourite establishment for tea. It was touching when John, the owner of a souvenir stall in Piccadilly, asked where my mum was. When I stated she had died, John said that he had enjoyed talking with her over the years. Comfort will come in expected places and times.

Was there something on your loved one's Bucket List that they did not get to see or accomplish? My mother had wanted to do a certain holiday cruise around New Zealand, but ran out of time. We got an unbelievable price and took it in her memory. I won a future cruise in Holland America's raffle! Some women have done charity runs and climbs for family members who have survived or succumbed to a certain disease.

34

Dating Post-Divorce

Do a Self-Assessment First

When one has been in a long-term marriage, it can be daunting jumping back into the dating pool again. How does one begin? Online dating sites, blind dates or the new trend of group dating? Before even starting, be clear about who you really are and your values. Do you feel like a fragment and only whole if in a relationship? Do you lose your sense of self and become merely a reflection of your mate? A way to avoid facing one's own flaws is to adopt someone else's interests, values, and view-points. Take a breather after divorce to regroup. If you want to be around positive, kind people, then be that yourself.

Take stock of your requirements in potential partners to see what is fantasy and what is realistic. Make a list of these qualities by order of importance to see if some of the trivial ones at the bottom can be eliminated. Wanting to be swept off your feet by a handsome guy to go traveling around the world may be realistic if you are a twenty-two year-old model, but less so if you are over fifty and not attracted to geriatrics. When several women were asked "What qualities do you have that would attract this type of fellow," they could only answer, "That is who I want." Think about what specific traits that you possess that would attract the type of mate you desire. If you are fuzzy, then consider talking to a dating coach to ease you back into the dating scene.

Are you too picky, wanting the same qualities that you looked for while in college? Some women have said that a guy has to be buff or drive a certain sports car. Another woman stated that a guy has to be over six feet, since she wears high heels. Are you bypassing Mr. Nearly Right for the elusive Mr. Right? No one is going to check all of your boxes. If there are no fireworks on the first date, then maybe a few more dates will show that there are some sparks. One may lose out on a fantastic guy or woman because some relationships grow in intensity over time.

Some people have left college or a parental home to get married and never lived on their own or discovered who they are and what makes them tick. Fear of loneliness and being on their own causes some to do serial dating. Serial dating is when one goes from person to person without a breather in between. Conquer loneliness first instead of grabbing someone to keep you amused. Consider adopting or fostering a cat or dog for company. My mother had the TV or radio on during the evenings so that she did not have a quiet house. Step out and meet new people, join groups and volunteer. Change your work schedule if it is more difficult to be home alone at a specific time of day. I felt more alone when married that I ever did post-divorce.

The Dos and Don'ts of Dating Again

It can be tricky going on first dates again. Having a professional make over can boost your confidence and ensure that your hair style is not a relic from the eighties. One divorced man has this sage advice when dating again. "Just put one foot in front of the other and keep on walking." He said to go through the motions of a date and then they get easier and easier.

Have a mental list of potential conversation topics or write some down to stash in your pocket for an emergency. People have said the usual ones, such as current movies, books, and news events are still good today, just as they were before marriage. One woman mentioned the added bonus of dating again in later life is having the topic of careers. There is much material to discuss and amusing anecdotes of co-workers to break the ice.

Having an interesting life gives one a sense of allure. Not only is conversation more stimulating, but can lead to more connections with dates. You may know mutual acquaintances in various venues or have participated in similar activities. My active friends with dynamic lives are full of stories and adventures whether or not they are formally employed. A person who keeps busy is more attractive to potential partners than someone whose bum warms the couch in the evenings.

There is a thing as too much information. One woman in a mixed group described all the extra mucous she now has in the morning since moving to a higher altitude. We all practically gagged. She wonders why she does not have second dates. Another acquaintance tells her life story too quickly, mistaking that as a way to have instant intimacy. Intimacy and other traits such as trust, build up over time, not in an hour. In a former job, a co-worker told extremely personal stories about people we did not even know. Who cares about her best friend's sex life? Guys may wonder what one is saying about them when secrets are spilled inappropriately. It is fine to be a bit mysterious, rather than being an open book too soon.

Be a good listener. People enjoy talking about themselves and usually appreciate the opportunity to do so. Ask questions that require an in depth answer, not simply yes or no. Make eye contact to show interest, but not constantly, which can be intimidating. I have found sitting a little more to the side rather than directly across from a guy can be more comfortable.

Another post-divorce dating concern is this. Do you follow a pattern of being with the same type of person? Is your soon-to-be-ex similar to former boy/girl friends? Deidre's father was a sociopath and she married one as well. Deidre's former fiancé also had his issues and problems. Her friends gently suggested that if she decided to date again, to be very careful and possibly see a counsellor.

A woman I met during my divorce recommends that divorcees wed widowers who have been happily married. As a veteran of a contemptuous divorce, she remarried one of these men and said that they "don't carry all of the baggage and bitterness" that many divorced men do the second time around. An added bonus is that she is not drawn into a battle with any exes. Juliette, a charming southern belle in her 60s, echoed this same sentiment. Juliette is blissfully wedded to a widower, who had been happily married the first time around.

Group Dating

Group dating can be less scary since you are not going it alone. Various dating sites have popped up globally with this new trend. One dating site has you bring two friends and it provides three of the opposite gender. The meeting place is in a public bar or restaurant where the host seats you three and brings the other ones to your table as each arrives. One person said that the whole place seemed to have been reserved for these groups of six. Part of the fee for this dating site, is for one round of drinks that is provided by the establishment. Even if you do not meet the love of your life, the evening sounds like a lot of fun.

Another dating site is for a dinner party for six at the host's home. People are strangers, but are chosen for compatibility. You would then host the next dinner party, inviting the former host. The dating site would send four others to your flat. There seems to be more security with a group date at your place. I have heard that some networking results from this process as well as future dates. Consider doing an online search for group dating web sites in your locale.

Speed dating is a way to meet many potential dates in a short period of time and not have to make decisions or face rejection on the spot. There are different venues that can be found online for your city. One can preregister for a certain age group and pay the fee. You can go by yourself or with friends to these events. They usually have the same number of genders. You have a specified period of time to talk with each person before a bell rings, somewhere between five to ten minutes. Take notes so you remember who you would like to meet again at a later time. Ask the same few questions with each person, so that you can make accurate comparisons. Then go into a conversation to see if there is an attraction. After the event, each person lets the organizers know who they are interested in seeing again. When a man and women select each other, then both are given a way to contact the other person through the organization. It takes a few days after the event before you receive any matches. This type of matchmaking takes the pressure off people so they can have some fun while encountering potential partners.

Online Dating

One woman went on a well-known dating site for six months and did not care for the potential dating pool. She felt that the people were weird. After switching to another popular one, she instantly met the man of her dreams and is close to getting engaged. She advises to try different dating sites, even if the one you are using is supposed to be great.

Do expect that there will be some disappearing acts. The dreaded words one heard in college, "I'll be in touch" can also mean the same today, that no future dates are happening. Just like in your earlier days, you have no clue why. A few women who live in small towns stipulate on their profiles that they only date fellows who live at least twenty miles away. When asked why, their answers were that they did not want to run into people locally, when dates bombed.

Do not give out personal contact information or take a new date home. A woman met a man online in Australia, who seemed compatible. When they got together in a public place, he gave her the creeps. She did want to be seen with him, so she took him to her house for a quick bite and sent him on his way. She refused future dates, which angered him, so he came back to her house at a later date and murdered her. Unfortunately, her four-year-old son witnessed this horrendous act, and also became motherless.

Dating sites may not do background checks, so be cautious that you are not meeting a criminal. The man that murdered the Australian woman had previously been in jail for a violent rape. Consider paying more for a match-making dating site that does an extensive interviews and background checks. One is also carefully matched for compatibility.

Problem: Why are there long dry spells between dates?

Solution: It takes practice in the dating scene to feel more relaxed and confidant.

• Make sure that your profile is accurate and that your photo is recent. Have a friend check your profile before it is posted. If online, maybe there is something in it that is turning people off, like a cutesy kitten photo or ambiguous wording that could be tweaked.

• Ask friends for their candid opinions about your hair, makeup and so forth. Males may want to consult their barber about updating their hairstyle. A personal stylist at a department store can be invaluable in updating your appearance and clothes.

• Consider going to a dating coach to help sort out why you are not having more than a couple of dates with a person. Are you revealing too much too soon, or talking about your ex? Your girlfriends and male buddies can give advice on what may be an issue in your dating realm. Listen carefully without getting defensive. Consider going on a double date with your pal and her husband, to get feedback on your dating interactions. Guys may want to ask their female co-workers for candid feedback on how they come across to women.

• Learn to recognize problems and foibles so that you do not have low expectations that lead to being a doormat. Did you live up to your potential in your marriage? If not, use this time to explore different areas of opportunity and fulfilment. Discover what brings joy and meaning to your life. Contemplate what you have learned from your marriage and take responsibility for your part in its demise so as not to repeat these mistakes again. You are free to pursue dreams that may have been put on the back burner during your marriage.

Red Flags on the Dating Scene

Problem: Differentiating between a dangerous vs. devoted person

Solution: One may have seen a dating or divorce coach to avoid repeating the same missteps that contributed to the demise of the marriage. One may have gained valuable insight on avoiding the same type of toxic person as their former spouse. Be careful when a new date seems too good to be true, because that very well could be the case. Trust your gut feeling if you seem uncomfortable or uneasy around this new person. Your subconscious may be trying to let you know that all is not as it seems. Listen to your body if you are feeling on edge, yet cannot determine why, when he seems so kind. Plenty of women and men have been swindled out of a chunk of cash by charming con artists.

• If the relationship is intense from the start with a lot of fireworks, this does not mean love at first sight. If the relationship is moving too quickly, apply the brakes. Relationships are not a race, but meander along to give both parties plenty of time to get to know each other. If you feel pushed for a commitment, just take your time. Ask to meet their family and friends to get a better picture of them. One divorced friend met a guy who got serious immediately, yet there were gaps of time that they were not together. Gale wanted to meet his family, but got excuses instead. They were on the verge of moving in together when she got a tearful phone call. His wife found out about Gale and begged her to let go of her husband since they had two small children. Gale was aghast that she had been duped by this charismatic man and promptly dumped him. If you are in a new relationship with someone and he is consistently unavailable on holidays and the weekends, it is a sign that he may be married. Does he always come over to your place, but has excuses about not going back to his? One guy complained that his "roommate" did not like company. This "roommate" turned out to be his wife.

• Does she borrow money, but not pay it back? Does he flit from job to job and blames his boss or co-workers when they do not work out for very long? Some people have opted to hire a private detective or do an online search when something seemed fishy with their new dating partner. These charming people will have an explanation about everything and do not like to be confronted with facts.

• Is he or she rude to waiters, salesclerks or other people that do not seem to matter? How do they treat others in general? Are they kind to animals? Assess if your ethics and values are similar. Listen to see if he makes racist or sexist remarks. He may be the type that uses people for his own gain and dismisses those that are of no use to him. There is truth to "Birds of a feather stick together." If you meet a guy, but he has friends who are disrespectful of women or animals, think again. This bloke may be covering up what he is really like in order to get closer to you. Maybe there is a darkness inside of him that attracts the same type of friends. Naomi was dating this very nice PhD-bound student from a loving family. She could just imagine them as in-laws and kept making excuses for some odd behaviours from her boyfriend. When Naomi pointed out inconsistencies, he always had a reason, and usually it was someone else's fault. Then Naomi took a hard look at her boyfriend's buddies. Some were out picking up girls while in committed relationships. She met his mentor professor, who was so into hardcore porn (before the Internet), that it slowly dawned on her what was transpiring, as her guy became more belittling and worse. It was difficult, but she broke up with him and learned to check out the people around potential boyfriends. Abigail Van Buren (Dear Abby) stated, "The best index to a person's character is how he treats people who can't do him any good and how he treats people who can't fight back."

• One may have worked through his or her own issues, but is oblivious that their partner is still carrying baggage from the first marriage. I went to visit my college roommate before her pending wedding. Her fiancé's first wife had cheated on him, resulting in their divorce. He barely wanted to let Cara out of his sight, except for when she was working. I had not seen her in some years, and was annoyed that we only had a quick dinner at a restaurant before Jim showed up to spend the rest of the evening with us. He obviously had a trust issue from his past marriage that was not resolved. This shows why premarital counselling is important before tying the knot again, especially when children are involved.

• On a darker note, men can prey on vulnerable women with low self-esteem, who can be controlled. When he wants to know a woman's every move and frequently calls to check on her whereabouts, that is not love but rather is emotional abuse. Bells may go off in your head if he then starts to segregate you from friends and family. If he wants you to drop people just to be with him, run the other way. This could escalate to physical abuse. No matter how sexy he is, get out of this relationship fast.

• A big red flag is when your friends and family do not like your new love interest and wonder if you have lost your mind. Put your ego in check and ask specifically what bothers them. They may have noticed some discrepancies (lies) and character flaws that you are glossing over. Go on a double date with a good friend and their spouse to get an honest assessment. Guys can see through other guys better than we can, and may have some useful observations. Women can suss out other women and see if she is a gold digger. It is better to break things off early when these red flags appear, than to keep giving more chances and end up with a broken heart.

Listen to your intuition

Maybe someone you meet reminds you of a difficult person you knew and alarm bells go off in your head. Well, listening to your intuition may prevent you from getting into a sticky situation. That person may remind you of someone else that you do not like because they share some of the other one's similar devious characteristics.

Trust your gut instinct when it tells you something different from your intellect. You may encounter a seemingly ethical person in business or the healing arts, but something just does not seem right. That person appears to be a caring soul, but you seem to feel a little on edge and do not know why. That is your gut instinct letting you know that there is something questionable going on, perhaps at a subconscious level.

You are more vulnerable during and when recently divorced, which may affect your judgment. Feel free to avoid or limit contact with people with whom you are uncomfortable. Forensic Files on TV is full of true stories about people who were too polite to say, "Good-bye." If you feel awkward around someone, then do not let them into your house, as one sister-in-law did. Her brother-in-law killed the woman, with her two young children present. She had told many people, including her parents, that she felt unsafe around this man. Another case was about a high school honour student who accepted a ride with a neighbour and never arrived home. Do not waste time or energy talking to these toxic people. It is not worth your safety to be polite.

35

Re-Marriage

Prenuptial Agreement

When you are ready to take the plunge and get married again, consider doing a prenuptial agreement to protect your assets. This legal contract drawn up by a lawyer, lists your individual assets, and how they will be dispersed in the event of divorce. This is especially important when there are offspring from a previous marriage and you do not want their future inheritance to be lost in a divorce. Although a prenup may stipulate the dispersion of property in death as well as divorce, this does not take the place of a will.

See if it is advantageous to have your current house or any other property put into a trust for your children. Money accumulated during a marriage is usually split upon divorce. If you rent out your house during your marriage, you both would benefit from the income it generates. You want to put in a prenup agreement that the house will remain in your possession if there is a divorce. A prenup can be invalidated if done too close to the wedding date (less than two months), or if it seems like one party was coerced into signing it. It is best for each person to have their own attorney check over this document before signing it. A future spouse probably knows that you had a divorce from Hell, and would want to prevent anything like that one occurring again.

Prenups are especially valuable when one partner has a business and does not want to lose all or part of it in divorce. Any income derived from the business during marriage is considered joint property. When there is a May-December romance, a prenup may be drawn up to give the woman a life-time interest in the house so she does not lose her home upon her husband's death. When she dies, the house may then pass on to the late husband's family.

Prenups are not just about financial matters. Some stipulate who does certain duties or household tasks. In an international marriage, one may designate which country they want for their children's residence. Others state what religion future children will have. What is put into a prenup is not always granted by a judge down the road, as is seen in some celebrity divorces. Some countries, such as England, are less apt to enforce a prenup agreement if it is deemed unfair to one of the parties. At least with a prenuptial agreement, each partner's wishes are clearly stated.

Dealing with Your Ex-spouse's Remarriage

When one is still mourning the divorce, it can be disconcerting to hear your former spouse is tying the knot again. Any hope for reconciliation is now dashed. You may be surprised at the intensity of emotions that bubble up with the imminent wedding of your ex. This can trigger feelings of rejection and illuminate one's lack of dates and relationships. Perhaps building connections to others can lessen feelings of abandonment that surfaced with the remarriage. Determine if it is the wedding itself that is upsetting or rather you have not yet found someone else and are lonely.

You may feel he or she caused so much hurt, that they do not deserve to be happy with someone else. It is challenging when one former partner has moved on and the other is wallowing in self-pity. Dwelling in the "what ifs" is not helpful, however analysing what went wrong –so as not to repeat them in subsequent relationships, can be. There is no time machine to transport you to the past, so do not revisit it. Banish thoughts of "If only I..." or "what if we had ..." It is over.

The key to getting through this episode in your life is distraction. Plan on doing something challenging to keep your mind occupied, such as skiing or other active sports. Moping around with nothing to do compounds misery. Enlist friends to take a day trip or other fun pursuits. This is the time to discover those far flung destinations on your Bucket List. Navigating the labyrinth of streets in Venice or getting lost in Paris will take your thoughts off his wedding day.

Acknowledge your sadness, process it and later express these thoughts with friends. Just do not dwell in these emotions which can affect your health and well-being. Some people have found that giving a shape to these feelings, such as balloons and visualizing their release, has aided in letting go. Consider seeing a divorce coach to get your life back on track. If feeling depressed, a therapist can be helpful with strategies and sorting out your situation. Do not suffer in silence.

If you have children, keep a neutral demeanor and do not share your feelings. They may want to take part in the nuptials, so be flexible if the wedding day falls during your shared time. Reassure the kids that you have your own plans, so that they do not worry about you on that day. If the youngsters feel that accepting a new step-parent is disloyal to you, then that causes stress for them. Be supportive to them and any new family members even if you have to grit your teeth. Some women remarked that their ex-spouse getting remarried was just the push that they required to move on. This was closure for the past and beginning the next chapter to start life anew.

Blended Families

A step-parent is not a parent replacement, but rather a special family friend that fills a unique niche. I could discuss almost anything with my step-mother and she was my go-to-person for questions on puberty. My divorced friend has been close to her ninety year old step-mother for decades. A step-parent's role is not as a go-between for the parents nor is it as a negotiator to settle their disputes.

This article is reprinted with permission from The Divorce Magazine, UK
By Wendi Schuller

A Guide for Blended Families

Step-parents and children can thrive in blended families with a little understanding of the process. Merging begins with the Courting Phase, just as with dating. People are on their best behaviour, showing their good side and hiding their less stellar points. They may be more giving than usual, saying "I'll take your glass to the sink, just sit there darling."

Then comes the Honeymoon Phase. The newly blended family is having extra fun, going to amusement parks and keeping occupied with other enjoyable pursuits. Life is one big holiday and individuals are getting along so well.

Then day to day reality sets in. Not only is the sink pointed out to the child, but so is the mop and dust cloth. Chores materialize and the honeymoon is over. Disenchantment can set in on both sides. The children may become sulky when life is no longer all fun and games. The step-parent wonders what happened to the sweet kids and who are these opinionated brats?

How to make blending go smoother? Be your authentic self at all times. Be warm and kind, but not bending over backwards to fulfil the children's every whim. From day one, let them know that there is no maid service, so everyone takes their glasses to the sink.

You are not their best friend and let them warm up to you on their own time schedule. Do not attempt to bribe them with presents to win them over. Even if they never come around completely, insist upon respect and good manners, not love. Let them know you are there for them, whenever they want help.

Realize that people are on their best behaviour during the Courting Phase, so do not be blindsided when reality sets in. Children can be great, but have to let off steam. Do not take it personally when it happens. Some of my friends have talked about their own step-mothers to their new step-children. They emphasize what great family friends they are and how they fill a special supportive role.

As a biological parent, consider having regular family meetings to air concerns and set up a rota for chores. My step-mother gave me chores to do when I came over on the weekends and this helped me to feel a part of her family. I felt like I did my share and was not a guest. Give expected behaviour guidelines, such as treating everyone with respect. Ask kids what special treats and fun they would like, but be clear that you are not getting a bank loan to do expensive activities every weekend. It was the little things that I enjoyed most with my step-mum, such as making paper dolls or baking brownies. One step-dad was great at helping his step-son maintain his clunker of a car. It is the experiences that are so meaningful to step-kids.

Expect bumps in the road. Life may be going smoothly, then there is chaos. This can be a result of children turning into teens or other issues. The key is communication. Attempt to discuss what is going on. If things become more difficult, consider a session or two with a divorce coach to get everyone back on track. One may discover that there are issues with the other parent or difficulties at school.

With time, blended families grow to love, or at least like each other. It was wonderful for me to gain an instant extended family, since I am an only child. It helps when the biological parent is supportive of the new step-parent, as my mother was of my step-mum.

36

Happiness and Meaning in Life

"The greater part of our happiness or misery depends upon our dispositions and not by our circumstances."
—Martha Washington

Viennese author Viktor Frankl was sent to a concentration camp with some family members and this ordeal is in his book, *Man's Search for Meaning*. While imprisoned, he discovered that others who found meaning in life were more apt to survive. Frankl stated that the Nazis could not take away one's attitude, one's outlook on life. He met several men who had given up and were waiting to die. Frankl delved into their lives and discovered that what was important to them was waiting on the outside. For one, it was a family member who was safely tucked away from harm, and the other had a project that had been left unfinished. These two men then became determined to live and they made it out of the concentration camp alive. The Center for Disease Control, (CDC) said that four out of ten Americans have not discovered their meaning in life, and that negatively affects their health.

What is the difference between just having happiness and having meaning/purpose in life? Happiness is more transient. You are happy because you have money to buy expensive the latest gadget or fashion piece. If something were to take those away, then your happiness would fade. Having meaning in life is more long-lasting. Frankl stated that the more one is focused outside of herself by reaching out to others, the more human you are.

Roads to happiness include having goals in life, delving into spirituality and doing community service. Having friends and social interactions increase one's happiness and the feeling of having meaning in one's life. There are ways to increase your happiness, such as doing good deeds every day and being thankful for what you have.

Increase your well-being after a court hearing or confrontation with your ex by doing a good deed for another. Allow a car, which has been waiting to enter a line of traffic, get in front of you. Return a shopping cart for an elderly person, after she has unloaded her groceries. Let a father with a cranky toddler get ahead of you in the grocery line. Their gratitude and smiles give your mood a positive boost and erase some irritations.

Since happiness is a more fleeting feeling there are ways to boost its level every day. Spend your money on experiences, rather than on more material goods. Travel opens one's eyes and mind to new cultures, sights, and ideas which is life changing. You bond with your kids and acquire lifetime memories. Having lattes with friends bi-weekly, tops up my happiness level. Make a list of what gives you pleasure and enjoyment. Then schedule these on a weekly basis in your calendar. Just thinking about what you were happy about that day can give you a more positive outlook on life. Jot down these happy thoughts in a journal.

The December, 2009 issue of Australia's *Women's Weekly* magazine presented research results on the topic of happiness. This magazine stated that studies on identical twins raised in different homes found that they "have similar levels of life satisfaction." The results suggested that there existed a genetic component to happiness. Some researchers stipulate that there is a "set point" of happiness.

We dip below this set point during troubling times, such as going through a divorce, but bounce back to this point at a later time. This explains why some people seem to see the world through rose coloured glasses, while others view it as the glass half empty.

Australian Professor Robert Cummins does not view this as a negative, but instead feels that we all operate on a particular level of happiness. He says that people "can build resilience to the knocks in life by marrying a supportive partner or having enough savings to weather a storm" when they have a lower set point of happiness.

You control your happiness and the meaning you find in life. A Buddhist proverb states "Pain is inevitable, but suffering is optional." Nelson Mandela could have languished and given up during his long prison term. People could not imprison his mind or spirit and he lived to fulfil his life mission of ending apartheid.

Australian Dr. Timothy Sharp says that happiness is in people's control, and research shows that we "can bump up our long-term happiness by having enriching relationships, developing goals and contemplating what we want out of life."

Buddhist philosophy says that when you are faced with adverse circumstances, feeling unhappy serves no purpose in overcoming the undesirable situation. Instead, it increases your anxiety. Anxiety and unhappiness affect your sleep patterns, your appetite and your health. If nothing can be done to resolve the difficulty (as in divorce situations), it is useless to feel unhappy about it.

Gratitude

Various people have commented on how powerful the act of gratitude is to one's well-being. Everyday write down a certain number (3 to 10) of things you are thankful for that happened that day. It does not matter how big or small these are. What this process does is to change your focus to the positives in your daily life. Your attention is drawn to what is pleasant, instead of dwelling on the negatives. After doing this for at least a week, I noticed that the flowers around my neighbourhood seemed brighter. I observed different birds and more butterflies. People appeared to be smiling at me more, or maybe I did not notice that as much earlier. It takes around three months for an action to become a habit. After practicing gratitude for that length of time, it becomes ingrained into your daily life.

Some women opt to take photos of what they are thankful for in their lives and keep them as reminders. This could be a luscious latte, as one woman did who was grateful for her local coffee shop. Many snapshots are of family pets or stunning sunsets. An activity in Australia which is gaining in popularity is to take pictures on a daily basis to remind people to pause and enjoy life.

Reflect on the small pleasures around you. I was walking around our neighbourhood with a friend and we stopped to enjoy an impromptu concert. A bird, sitting in the treetop, was singing her heart out with a beautiful melody. Any disappointments of that day were quickly forgotten and replaced with this lovely experience. My cats' antics brings laughter.

Secret to Longevity

There was a study done a few years back to see if feeling and acting younger impacted one's health. Men were divided into two groups and spent different weeks at a lodge. The control group watched current movies, TV shows and news, then discussed what was happening in their lives.

The other group of men had strict instructions to act as though they were living in a certain year, which was about 30 years in the past. The TV shows, movies and news broadcasts were just what would have been seen in that particular year. These men were only allowed to talk about their personal lives and world events from that year, or earlier. If they were dating then, that girl was discussed, but not their future marriage. These fellows talked about sports and other interests from that era.

Extensive blood work and tests were performed before and after the week at the lodge with both groups. The guys in the control group may have been a little more relaxed afterward, but significant medical changes were not found.

However, there was a measurable difference in the immune system, cardiac function, blood pressure and other body systems in the men who lived a week in the past. There was a marked decrease in arthritic pain and other complaints, with a surge in energy. The researchers said they were amazed by how much the health of the men had improved in the second group.

Get in touch with your younger self and remember your passions and interests. Watch those old reruns of your favourite TV shows and talk about the good old times with your pals. Notice your increase in energy and how those aches and pains diminish. One article that I read recently stated that those people who feel younger actually can increase their lifespan by ten years.

37

Moving On

Forgiveness

Forgiveness is about setting yourself free, not about the other person. You forgive and do not have to let the other person know that you did so, or even see him again. It is about cutting free any ties that bind you to certain situations or people and letting go of the past. Visualize a matrix where you are connected to your ex. Now see a large pair of scissors cutting through every string that binds you to him. Notice the feeling of lightness when no ties of resentment are attaching you to each other. I repeated this daily during my divorce and sporadically afterwards.

You have read in the papers how parents have forgiven their child's murderer, and you probably wondered if they were saints or nuts. What these parents did was to let go of bitterness, anger and any other attachments, so that they could get over this tragedy and move on with their lives. Dr. Carl Simonton, of the Simonton Cancer Center in California, stated that not forgiving others can lead to an "increased risk for cancer." Holding onto a grudge is dangerous for your health, such as by raising ones blood pressure. It also restricts blood flow and oxygenation, which worsens chronic pain and increases headaches."

Natalie's mother did not forgive her ex-husband and was bitter for decades. When Natalie got a divorce, it was a trigger for her mother to relive her own divorce experience.

She had a heart attack followed by a stroke. Natalie learned from her mother's example and decided to forgive her former spouse to prevent future health issues and to live a more fulfilled life.

Webster's Dictionary defines "forgiveness" as "To cease to feel resentment against one's enemies." Not forgiving is a way to stay attached to your ex and remain stuck in resentment and bitterness. Not forgiving is maintaining a tie to him and leaves you shut off to future relationships. Forgiveness severs the hurt/injustice which binds you both together. Forgiveness is just about letting go and not about getting revenge. Thoughts of revenge keep you connected to that person.

Archbishop Desmond Tutu said that "chains of bitterness" keep us bound to the one who hurt us, who is our jailor. When we forgive that person "we take back control of our own fate" essentially breaking out of this prison to be free.

Angela feels that divorce helped her learn how to forgive, which has been beneficial in other situations in her life. When a co-worker is petty, or a family member annoying, she does not dwell on this. She forgives and moves on. No, Angela does not agree with these actions, but forgives these people to "keep looking forward and not backward."

What helped me with the first step of forgiving my ex was remembering times when I said mean things to others or was not kind. Knowing that I make my share of mistakes made it easier to forgive my ex. People mess up, and it is the enormity of these mistakes that is different. Self-forgiveness was necessary first, before being able to forgive others.

It is important to forgive yourself, so that you can heal and move on, and not remain mired in the past. You did the best that you could with the life skills and knowledge that you possessed at that time. Louise L. Hay has a great book, *The Power is Within You*, which teaches you how to forgive yourself and others and not repeat destructive patterns of your past. She recommends saying to yourself, "I'm doing the best that I can and even though I'm in a pickle now, I will get out of it somehow, so let's find the best way to do it."

Affirmations

Author Catherine Ponder in her book, *Open Your Mind to Prosperity*, recommends saying this affirmation to help let go of toxic people or situations: "I now release and am released from everything and everybody that are no longer part of the Divine Plan for my life. Everything and everybody that are no longer part of the Divine Plan for my life now release me." What is nice about this affirmation is that it is a two way street, because you are stating for your ex to cut ties with you as well. I wrote this on a coloured index card with a vibrant felt pen and propped it up by my bathroom mirror, so I could say this several times a day. I still revisit this affirmation when angry thoughts about my ex pop up out of nowhere.

Affirmations are positive statements that you can make about what you want out of life in a myriad of situations. What you are doing is working with your subconscious mind and a Higher Power (whatever is in your belief system) to move you towards change. Any Catherine Ponder book is chock full of affirmations that I tweak to fit my individual situation. You can make specific ones, such as about your next court date having a positive outcome or that you get "xyz" with the property division. Some affirmations that worked for me are:

271

"Divine guidance is now showing me the way to... (insert your situation, such as an amicable divorce). Divine Guidance is working through me and all concerned to bring about the perfect outcome now." "All financial doors are open to me now and are manifesting abundance in expected and unexpected ways. God is bringing me wealth and opportunities and I give thanks for them."

Forgiveness is the first step to change. Understanding and love come after this, so that destructive patterns of the past can be altered or eliminated.

A great life guide is the Law of Karma, which is the law of cause and effect, not punishment. It parallels biblical verses, such as "What you sow, so shall you reap." Another is, "What goes around comes around," and also The Golden Rule. If your gossip and actions cause misery for others, do not be surprised when misery comes knocking on your door. Allow Karma to do its thing, not you. It is not in your job description to mete out punishment.

Revenge is hatred in action. Retaliation leads to progression and can escalate quickly. Nip any revenge thoughts in the bud, or they can block you from leaving your current situation to move on. When someone has dealt you a cruel blow, do not plot revenge. You have heard of road rage, where people want to dish out revenge on the spot, sometimes with fatal results. It is karma that will come back to you and not add to your happiness.

Think of the cliché, "It's like water rolling off a duck's back," and let those insults roll off you. It is not worth having a stroke or a heart attack to prove that you are right. Your body responds to thoughts and images as if they were real. When one starts feeling upset about injustice and plots punishment to the perpetrator, then the blood pressure and heart rate rises. This can lead to a headache or exacerbate a medical condition. Save your health and realize that they are the ones with problems. Use this affirmation: "Divine Justice is doing its work in this situation now."

When people move across the country to get away from problems, in reality they are packing these woes with them. Life will keep repeating the same experiences or types of relationships until we master that lesson and move on. Here are some questions to ask yourself: Do you accept personal responsibility or is it always someone else's fault? Are you focused on spiritual growth or selfish gain? Are you ruled by monetary goals and instant gratification? Do you learn from your personal history?

Helion Publishing produces wonderful credit card-size cards of information on many different subjects, such as karma and even reflexology that can act as daily reminders to support positive behaviour.

38

Post-Divorce Advice and Guidance

Notify acquaintances of your new post-divorce status when you bump into them, if you prefer not to make a general announcement. I would immediately tell people I had not seen in a while that I was happily divorced, revealing how my sons' lives were wonderful. If strange looks were given, I would proceed to relay that my sons gave me flowers and chocolates on my divorce anniversary. A few women babbled, "I am so sorry," and I would ask them whatever for, since I just said how much better my sons and I are doing post-divorce.

If you are grieving or upset, a simple, "We got divorced. How are you?" will suffice. You do not owe anyone an explanation or graphic details regarding your divorce situation. Smile and remark, "I have moved on," whether or not you really have.

A few divorced pals have made some radical changes in their appearance to start this new chapter in life. Some men and women decided to forgo the grey hair and got new styles and colours. I had a department store makeover and learned a few more techniques and added another product which produced a more professional appearance. I found that Neal's Yard skin care in Frankincense makes my skin glow. Another divorced friend discovered the joy of professionally applied gel nail polish and is proud of her manicures. Some are deliberating the pros and cons of cosmetic procedures as they jump back into the dating pool.

Others have started using anti-aging potions post-divorce to banish wrinkles. This could be the time to add a classic or trendy new piece to your wardrobe. I recently found a line of slim jeans that are more stylish than my former matronly ones.

Gail said "I never felt as beautiful as I did after my divorce. I lost twenty-five pounds without trying, and coloured my hair. People kept telling me how great I looked. During my divorce I felt like a worm." Gail is one of the happiest, most vivacious people that I know.

Financial

Post-divorce, develop a budget, even if it is the first time that you have ever done so. Keep an expense diary to see where every penny goes for at least two weeks. Look at your alimony and salary to set up a reasonable budget with a savings plan. By examining your financial diary, it will make it easier to see where to cut out some expenses. This may be the time to do a consultation with a financial adviser that charges a set fee for service, rather than a commission. Some less ethical advisers pick investments that give themselves more money, rather than what is best for you, the client. I had a stock broker working mainly on commission, who picked out a lousy annuity, because she got more money for it. The financial adviser can look at your expense diary and help you pinpoint where your money is going, plus devise savvy money-saving strategies.

I selected a financial company that has low administrative costs and does not pay multi-million dollar salaries or bonuses to the top tier for my investments post-divorce. I put part of my retirement into a "Target Date Fund" which matures near my possible retirement. This type of fund invests aggressively with a portfolio higher in stocks initially. Then it changes to a more conservative fund with less risk, but less growth nearer to its maturity date. The other pot for my retirement is a traditional IRA and ROTH IRA. Diversifying investments decreases the chance of losing a lot with a volatile market.

Financial Fasting works much like a diet fasting, where one reduces calories for a day or two a week. Fasting can be short-term, such as when one wants to lose a few pounds before a special event, or it can be life-long. Think of your finances in a similar vein. UK's *Women & Home* magazine's August 2013 issue had an article describing this new trend. Cut down on expenses for one or two days a week and spend your normal amounts on the other days. This will get you ahead in the financial game and put some extra cash in your pocket.

One may want to have a designated time frame for this Financial Fast with an option to extend it. The article suggested viewing the Financial Fast as a trade. You are giving up some extra frivolous expenditures for something that you really value, such as a trip or paying off the mortgage. My sons and I go to coffee shops or take walks on our fasting days. Others opt to bring their lunch to work or leave the credit card at home. Give this Financial Fast a go to see your dreams reached a little quicker. An Arabian proverb states that "If you only have two coins, spend one on food and the other one on flowers. One nourishes your body and the other one, your soul."

Post-Divorce Support

One may have been in a divorce or parenting group during this life transition. After the divorce has been finalized, sometimes we still need a bit of support and miss not being in a group setting. There are various organizations that provide assistance post-divorce to parents and children. One global organization is *Divorce Care* which meets weekly and shows a "video seminar" followed up by a discussion. Participants learn practical tips to help them recover from divorce and "ways to restore your hope and rebuild your life." What is nice about this organization is that some branches have children's groups for those aged 5 to 12 and are called *Divorce Care 4 Kids*. As stated earlier, UK's Maypole Women has helpful resources for the post-divorce period.

Restored Lives "supports and empowers people to move forward from divorce...to live a full life free from past issues." This UK charity has group sessions run by divorced people. The sessions start with a meal followed by discussions in small groups. The UK charity *Divorce Recovery* (DRW) workshops is mostly staffed by divorced volunteers. The six week sessions are two hours long and cover such topics as "Coping with your ex-spouse." DRW teaches "recovery from traumatic experiences can bring opportunities for personal growth." Americans also can enjoy the quarterly divorce weekend retreats in lovely country hotels.

Parents without Partners has meetings and social events in chapters across the US and Canada. In England, *Gingerbread* offers assistance for lone parents in getting benefits, finding childcare or employment.

Aguila Care Trust (TACT) has a network of self-help groups in the UK which offers "support, understanding and guidance of people struggling to put their lives together after divorce..." TACT first offers an eight week series of small group sessions followed by social events and workshops. The non-profit *National Council for the Divorced & Separated,* offers socials for divorced people in the UK, to "forget about their troubles for a couple of hours."

The Women's Center in the Washington D.C. area also has post-divorce services, including career advice and financial counselling. One of their classes is "Cover Letter Workshop – Getting Your Foot in the Door."

Do an online search or ask people what post-divorce resources are available in your community. Women's centres and the YWCA sometimes have workshops to get past divorce or other life traumas. Remember Meetup.com has specific divorce and single parent groups, particularly in larger cities like London or New York City.

Closure with Divorce

It is important to signify your divorce through an action for closure. One woman threw her wedding band into a fast moving stream which quickly swept it away. She felt a release and was able to get on with her life. Another had her wedding rings from two previous marriages melted down and made into a nice pendant. With other life transitions there are specific rituals to mark or celebrate them. This is lacking after divorce without a rite. People go through graduation ceremonies or attend a wedding reception. Death is followed by a funeral, yet there is nothing after a divorce. A few women reported having a complete makeover after divorce to close that chapter of their lives and embark on a new one. After we signed our divorce papers in my lawyer's office I felt like there should have been champagne. Plan something to mark the end of your marriage and new entry into single life, whether it is a luncheon with the girls or a sports match with the guys.

I decided to get a "divorce ring." I had a loose gemstone mounted in a ring that I designed and designated as my divorce one. The shop owners liked the concept tremendously and started to promote this trend. Some others have reset their engagement and wedding gems into new jewellery pieces. Yes, some divorces are sad events, leaving broken hearts, but others are "I'm so glad I escaped" ones.

A new trend is celebrating your divorce with a party. One photo in the news pictured a tiered cake with a bride on top and a groom at the bottom. Where I live, more and more people are having blow out parties to celebrate their divorces. One ex-wife hired a limo to take her girlfriends to a nearby city to party until the wee hours of the morning. After my divorce was finalized, my friends took me out for lattes or lunches over the following two months. My out-of-town-pals sent me cards to commemorate this happy occasion. Some fellows get together for beer and snooker or pool.

Some women are recipients of a "Divorce Shower" which can replace goods lost in their divorce or new pampering spa items are given. Divorce themed paper goods are available online for this occasion.

Wisdom Gained Post-Divorce

Many have had people and support on this journey to divorce. Emma Pritchard stated in the November, 2011, *Woman and Home Magazine*, "People always see divorce as a negative experience, but for me it's liberating. It's given me the confidence to achieve things I'd never imagined." Gina wished she had known she would emerge stronger after going through the turmoil of divorce. This is like metal becoming stronger after going through fire in the process of becoming a sword. Other friends echoed Gina's sentiment that they felt stronger, more empowered, and ready to tackle the world.

Resilience is another quality that people gain through divorce. Some revealed that no matter what life throws at them, divorce prepared them for anything. My Qi Gong instructor says to be flexible and bend like a pine tree, rather than being too rigid and breaking in a storm like an oak. Many stated that they learned patience, since divorce can be a long process, and this has carried over to different areas in life.

Friends have commented on the wisdom attained through divorce, which propelled them into new fields. Some followed passions that had been suppressed during turbulent marriages and now enjoy their creative careers. Others became more independent post-divorce and found it liberating to be on their own. I learned a few DIY skills and boast about them to my friends' husbands.

I hope this book enables you to gain insight on many issues that may have plagued you for years. It spells out how destructive ideas and actions can directly affect your health and well-being, providing a blueprint for self-change. Specific strategies are given for dealing with many aspects of your divorce, from obtaining cash and slashing costs to dealing with relationships. Relationships are not static, but change with divorce, and you can only alter your own actions, not someone else's behaviour. You are stronger than you envision, and if you follow some of the suggestions offered here, you will emerge from this stressful episode of your life as a more powerful person. Divorce is the catalyst for making changes in your life.

39

Checklist of Records and Information Needed by Attorney:

Name
Address
Your social security number
Your spouse's social security number
You and your spouse's social security report for projected retirement income
How long you have lived in this state/province/county?
Which country were you born?
Which country was your spouse born?
Marriage date
Separation date
Who is living in the marital home?
Was there a pre-nuptial agreement?

Children's names, ages, birthdates, social security numbers

Children are living with whom?

Your employment and starting date
Your spouse's employment and starting date

History of marriage
Any prior marriages for either spouse?

Any children from previous relationships from either spouse?
Are they receiving child support?
Are you currently in marital counselling?
Any history of marital abuse?
Any treatment for addictions?
Any police records for either spouse?
Are you pregnant?
Any health issues/disease/medical condition for spouses or children?
Any mental illness or diagnosed personality disorder?
Any conditions requiring long-term care?
Any disability for spouses or children?

Children's social security numbers
Children's bank account numbers and balance
Any 529 or educational plans?
Any treasury bonds for children? List numbers, amounts and maturity dates.

Income tax records for last 3 to 5 years

Bank accounts with numbers and balances
Joint
Yours
Spouse's

Any treasury bonds? List numbers, balance and maturity dates
Joint
Yours
Spouse's

List stock

Certificate numbers and amount of shares
In whose name?
Joint

Any bonds or other investments? List amounts
Joint
Yours
Spouse's

Retirement accounts

IRA/ROTH/ISA
Other
Any retirement plan tied to employer, where employer also
contributes to it?
Pension Plans
SEP accounts
Annuity Plans
In whose name?
Joint

Life insurance? Cash value of it? In whose name?
Any medical savings accounts?
Trusts?
Any other asset?

Credit cards with balances owed
Joint
Yours
Spouse's

Real Estate with address
Joint
In either spouses' names

Mortgage amount owed? Payoff date? In whose name?
Monthly mortgage?
Any liens on property?
Do you rent? Monthly amount

What debts are owed?
Any student loans? For whom?
Balance, maturity date and monthly payment for student loans.

Any promissory notes?
Any car loans? Monthly payment, balance owed and maturity date? For whose car?
Any business or personal loans?
Any personal debts to another person?
Any gambling debts?

Bring financial records including what assets you brought into the marriage

Any financial records showing parents paid credit card bills or part of house down payment?
Did any parent give financial assistance and will be paid back during divorce?
Any other financial issue that needs to be addressed in divorce?

Note any specific information requested by your lawyer

Notes

40

Recommendations and Links to Resources

Recommended Reading and Movies

Magazines:

My favourite magazines are *Woman and Home* and the *British Good Housekeeping*. There is a lot less fluff in these British ones and more practical advice than in many other magazines. They have inspiring articles on how women survived adversities and are now thriving. I also have a subscription to *The Australian Women's Weekly Magazine* for the same reasons, plus it is fun to get different viewpoints. Authors Professor Robert Cummins and Dr. Timothy Sharp write for *Australian Women's Weekly Magazine*. Lucy Beresford and Nicole Prieur are in UK's *Psychologies Magazine*. Emma Pritchard writes for *Woman and Home*. I especially enjoy reading these foreign magazines before holidays to discover their rituals and recipes. It is my splurge.

Additional informative magazines that provide insight and guidance are also listed below:

Woman and Home, British Edition published by IPC Media, Ltd.

The Australian Women's Weekly, published by ACP Magazines, a division of Nine Entertainment Co.

Good Housekeeping, British Edition, published by The National Magazine Company, Ltd. *Psychologies-UK*, Published by Hearst Magazines UK, trading name of the National Magazine Co. Ltd.

Red UK Edition, Hearst Magazines UK is the trading name of the National Magazine Company, Ltd.

O, The Oprah Magazine, published by Harpo Productions

Real Simple, published by Time, Inc., Lifestyle Group

Whole Living, published by Martha Stewart Living Omni Media, Inc.

Books:

These books are informative and can point you in the right direction:

Buchan, Elizabeth. *Revenge of the Middle Age Woman.* Penguin, 2003.

Ponder, Catherine. *Open Your Mind to Prosperity.* Marina Del Rey: DeVorss & Co. Publisher, 1971.

Ponder, Catherine. *The Prosperity Secrets of the Ages.* Marina Del Rey: DeVorss & Co. Publisher, 1964.

Ponder, Catherine. *The Healing Secrets of the Ages.* Marina Del Rey: DeVorss & Co. Publisher, 1967.

Ponder, Catherine. *The Dynamic Laws of Healing.* Marina Del Rey: DeVorss & Co. Publisher, 1966.

Hay, Louise L. *The Power is Within You.* Carlsbad, CA: Hay House, Inc.,1991.

Hill, Napoleon. *Think and Grow Rich*. Hollywood, CA: Wilshire Book Co.,1937.

Peale, Norman Vincent. *The Power of Positive Thinking*. New York: Simon & Schuster, 1952.

Grants, Corrine. *Lessons in Letting Go: Confessions of a Hoarder*. Published by Allen & Unmin, 2010.

Any financial book by Suze Orman which is published by Three Rivers Press in New York.

Helion Publishing, Box 52836, Tulsa, OK 74152 They produce wonderful credit card size information on a variety of subjects, such as karma.

Movies:

These movies are fun to watch and you can learn a few pointers from them.

"The Odd Couple" 1968.
"The First Wives Club," 1996.
"Nine to Five," 1980.
"The War of the Roses," 1989.
"Starting Over," 1979.
"Kramer vs. Kramer," 1979.
"Enough Said," 2013.

Watch any comedies, such as: "Tootsie," "If it's Tuesday it Must be Belgium," "It's a Mad Mad Mad Mad World," Laurel and Hardy, "The Wedding Singer" and whatever else tickles your fancy.

Online Media Resources:
http://www.thedivorcemagazine.co.uk/

http://www.divorcemag.com/
http://divorcedmoms.com/
http://www.divorcedigest.com/
http://www.maypole.org.uk/
http://nextchapter4women.com/
Divorce Support Organizations:
Divorce Care is a global organization that has branches in the US, UK and elsewhere. People learn practical tips that help them recover from divorce. Some branches of this organization have kids groups for those aged 5-12 and are called Divorce Care for Kids (DC4K). Divorce Care's web site is www.divorce.org

Relate offers "a range of services to help you if you're going through separation or divorce." http://www.relate.org.uk/

Routrouvaille It is for couples with marital problems including those who are considering marriage separation and those who are already separated or divorced that want marriage help. http://retrouvaille.org/

The Women's Centres have two locations in the Washington D.C. area and provide counseling and classes for those getting a divorce and moving on. www.thewomenscenter.org

From the decision to divorce to the future you deserve, & all the steps in between. Because how you divorce really does make a difference divorcesupportnet.com

Visions Anew provides workshops and classes for those facing divorce in Atlanta and Marietta
Email: info@visionsanew.org

The Lilac Tree: Resources for Divorcing Women near Chicago **thelilactree**.org

http://HopeAfterDivorce.org is our new website filled with excellent DIVORCE resources, community forum, panel of experts, a shop offering products. There is HOPE

We are here to help answer the many questions about the divorce process – from financial, to legal, to emotional. http://www.womens-divorce.org

A Better Divorce is a group of professionals committed to non-court solutions for family law matters & hoping to educate the public on non-adversarial options **A Better Divorce** _@A_Better Divorce

Aquila Care Trust
The Aquila Care Trust (TACT) is a growing network of self-help groups in UK founded in 1991 for the support, understanding and guidance of people struggling to put their lives back together after divorce Email: aquilaTrust@aol.com

Divorce Recovery Workshop
DRW is a UK nationwide self-help group run by volunteers who have personally experienced a relationship break-up. It aims to enable people to better understand what they are going through, provides them with support from others in the same situation and assists in the process of readjustment in their lives. www.drworg.uk/

Gingerbread
A support organisation for lone parents (through bereavement, divorce, www.gingerbread.org.uk

National Council for the Divorced and Separated

A voluntary group of people who know what it is like when you have lost a partner whether through divorce or any other reason. www.ncdsw.org.uk/

Parents without Partners is the largest international, nonprofit membership organization devoted to the welfare and interests of single parents and their children.
http://www.parentswithoutpartners.org/

The Parent Connection

Get expert divorce and separation advice including help on divorce with children involved, family mediation and co-parenting http://theparentconnection.org.uk/

Our Parenting Spot is an online site that features a forum for parents, plus information
http://ourmomspot.net/community/index.php